Contemporary
Central
American
Fiction

"Browitt's study proposes creative readings and interpretations of what he calls his 'affective corpus,' a collection of Central American short stories and novels written by male and female authors. The book explores what is left after the collapse, failure, and breakdown of patriarchal logic/thought in the public and private sphere, that is, bodies and affects. Truly innovative and an untouched territory in Central American literary criticism, Browitt complements this concentration on affects with a fine aesthetic sensibility, remaining receptive to the texts' literary quality and depth, to textual whisperings that prevent closure. Browitt delivers a complex and impassioned reading of texts that should be of utmost interest to students and critics of Central American literature."

Magdalena Perkowska, Professor Spanish and Latin American Studies, Graduate Center, Hunter College CUNY

"This book takes a fresh look at post-civil war Central American fiction of the last two decades. Browitt grasps the aesthetic registers that take us beyond the alienation of its characters to a range of post-national, fluid and nomadic sensibilities that defy or elude the failed heroic agency of the immediate past. The great value of this book is to witness the artful sensibility of the critic, who acknowledges and centers on the affect that these works generate. His readings are a reminder that art is not simply a reference to prevailing ideological interpretations of reality but a mobilizer of different imaginaries and sensibilities within ourselves."

George Yudice, Professor of Latin American Studies, University of Miami

Contemporary Central American Fiction

Gender, Subjectivity and Affect

JEFFREY BROWITT

sussex
ACADEMIC
PRESS
Brighton • Portland • Toronto

2 4 6 8 10 9 7 5 3 1

First published in hardcover 2018, and reprinted in paperback 2018, in Great Britain by
SUSSEX ACADEMIC PRESS
PO Box 139
Eastbourne BN24 9BP

Distributed in North America by
SUSSEX ACADEMIC PRESS
ISBS Publisher Services
920 NE 58th Ave #300, Portland, OR 97213, USA

British Library Cataloguing in Publication Data
A CIP catalogue record for this book is available from the British Library.

Library of Congress Cataloging-in-Publication Data
Names: Browitt, Jeff, author.
Title: Contemporary Central American fiction : gender, subjectivity and affect / Jeffrey Browitt.
Description: Includes bibliographical references and index.
Identifiers: LCCN 2017043012 | ISBN 9781845198602 (hbk : alk. paper)
ISBN 9781845199142 (pbk : alk. paper)
Subjects: LCSH: Central American fiction—20th century—History and criticism. | Central American fiction—21st century—History and criticism. | Family in literature. | Sex role in literature. | Subjectivity in literature. | Reality in literature. | Affect (Psychology) in literature. | Human-animal relationships in literature.
Classification: LCC PQ7472.N7 B76 2018 | DDC 863/.6099728—dc23
LC record available at https://lccn.loc.gov/2017043012

Typeset and designed by Sussex Academic Press, Brighton & Eastbourne.

Contents

Contents

PART III Gendered Bodies and Affects

Acknowledgments

I first went to a Central American literary conference in Antigua, Guatemala in 2000. I was encouraged to go by a then colleague at Monash University, Jorge Paredes, of Salvadoran background. I am forever thankful for his encouragement. I have returned nearly every year for the last seventeen years. I became captivated by the literature of the region, but just as importantly, by the people. It is the lasting friendships I have made with other Central America literary critics which keeps me returning year after year.

This book is deeply indebted to two people who have supported me in the project and read progressive drafts: Werner Mackenbach and Alexandra Ortiz Wallner. As experts in the field of Central America literary criticism, their advice and encouragement has been crucial. I am also indebted to Jessie Álvarez, Mauricio Chaves, Geannini Ruiz and Maybell Vargas Zúñiga for helping me locate copies of some of the texts studied here. Central American literature continues to suffer from poor distribution networks and lack of sufficient translations into other languages. In part, this book is designed to draw more attention within English-language reading circles to the literary production of the region. My critical approach is also in debt to the literary criticism that has gone before me and the contemporary criticism with which I am in constant dialogue. I am grateful, in particular, to a wonderful collective experiment in Central American literary criticism, and later cultural criticism, which manifested in the development of an online journal, *Istmo.Revista virtual de estudios literarios y culturales centroamericanos*, which was first launched in 2001, as well as the transdisciplinary and inter-institutional research program, 'Hacia una historia de las literaturas centroamericanas' (HILCAS), and the biennial *Congreso Centroamericano de Estudios Culturales*, which was first held in San Salvador in 2007. It has been a privilege to be involved in all projects. All these initiatives have given coherence to the field of

vii

Central American literary and cultural criticism, providing an outlet for regional intellectual production as well as forging durable networks of exchange and collaboration. I have benefited greatly from being part of a group of generous scholars that perhaps more than any other have been driving Central American literary criticism for the last twenty years. Their names are too numerous to mention — you know who you are. Take a bow.

I give special thanks to my immediate family. My partner Nidia Castrillón and my daughter Helen Browitt have been generous and understanding over the years as I have obsessed with academic life and Central American fiction in particular. Nidia has been both my immediate sounding board as well as a proof reader of my Spanish when I have published in the original language of the literature. Her presence in the book is unmarked, but deeply present — partners in life, partners in intellectual conversation. Helen has always been my 'tech guy' and just being around has made for a happy house and a positive environment in which to work. Finally, I would like to acknowledge the unstinting support of UTS library staff in procuring novels, short stories and books of criticism relevant to the region's literary work, without which this book would have taken much longer to produce.

Earlier and much shorter versions of the first three chapters of this book appeared in two publications in the online scholarly journal *Istmo* as 'Exorcizando los fantasmas del pasado nacional: *Got seif de Cuin!* de David Ruiz y *Margarita, está linda la mar* de Sergio Ramírez' (*Istmo* 3, January-June, 2002); and 'Managua, Salsa City: *El detrito de una revolución en ruinas*' (*Istmo* 15, July-December, 2007). I would like to thank the publishers for permission to re-work and extend these early essays and re-publish them in English. Permission was also granted by the Latin American Studies Association to briefly re-use some of the material from my memoir, 'On Becoming a Latin American Literary Critic' (LASA *Forum* 14: 2, 2014).

'Beyond here lies nothin',
but the mountains of the past.'
BOB DYLAN

For my parents,
Helen Walmsley and Cornelius Browitt

Introduction

'The text produces, in me, the best pleasure if it manages to make itself heard indirectly; if, reading it, I am led to look up often, to listen to something else.'

ROLAND BARTHES[1]

I once had the pleasure of lunching with the Guatemalan writer Rodrigo Rey Rosa in Berlin. In the course of conversation I pointedly asked him: 'Do you think Central American literary criticism is at the level of the fiction it analyses?' His answer was swift and minimal: 'No'. In one sense, then, this collection of critical essays on Contemporary Central American fiction is an attempt to respond to Rey Rosa's challenge. It is for the reader to decide on its merits. What I have tried to do is be creative with my critique without being trapped in the strait jacket of authorial intention and to dialogue critically with that fiction which has caught my interest, whether for philosophical, ethical, artistic or political reasons. The readings are not meant to be definitive, quite the opposite — they are meant merely as a contribution to a collective debate on a region's literature and, hopefully, a point of departure for others to challenge and create their own novel studies.

The book is a series of critical meditations on short stories and novels from Central America between 1995 and 2016. Literary art in Central America, as in Latin America in general, was strongly over-determined by the politics of the Cold War, which gave rise to popular struggle and three major armed civil wars in the 1970s and 1980s in Nicaragua, El Salvador and Guatemala. The impact of the conflicts reached into neighbouring countries like Costa Rica and Honduras. The period produced intense literary activity, with political ideology central and personified by the canonization of social denunciation in both the testimonial novel and revolutionary poetry. Throughout this period other forms of writing tended to be marginalised from critical attention.[2] During the armed conflicts and in the decade or so following the post-war period, the psychology of ex-combatants (guerrillas and soldiers) and dictators became dominant themes in Central American literature, certainly in its marketing and critical reception internationally. Since then, though themes of violence are still at much of its core, Central American fiction has become more complex. We have witnessed a resurgence of literary writing and criticism with a focus squarely on the artistic side of narrative art: writing aware of its own figurative manoeuvres and inventiveness, its philosophical and affective dimensions, and its carefully crafted syntax. Central American fiction now represents a virtual laboratory of fictional writing, daring in its subject matter and plots and nuanced in its fine-grained expression of both sociality and intimacy in the respective countries in which the fictions are generated. We can attribute nihilism or cynicism to the post-civil war writers for breaking with the great abandoned utopias, but the break has also led to a resurgence of literary democracy — writing no longer bound by expectations of a committed art but rather art period, by the desire for the exploration of intimacy and subjectivity, especially the type produced in the Central American urban space, which has as much or more importance for writers and readers than a *literature engagée*. The committed literature is there, but referenced obliquely and standing back from preaching. Though the peace accords did not bring the deep structural changes that the majority of Central Americans were hoping for, the space of artistic and literary freedom and experimentation has widened.

This collection of essays attempts to trace some of the contours of this new literature through close readings of fiction by Guatemala's Rodrigo Rey Rosa, Eduardo Halfon and Denise Phé-Funchal; Nicaragua's Franz Galich and Sergio Ramírez; Belize's David Ruiz Puga; El Salvador's Jacinta Escudos and Claudia Hernández; and Costa Rica's Carlos Cortés. It runs parallel with the constitution of new subjectivities and new sensibilities as fiction moves from the rural to the city, from the public to the intimate, from taken-for-granted, stable selfhood to more nomadic and fluid subjectivities, from the national to the post-national, and from utopian longings to abjection. This regional affect is linked to mourning for the revolutionary subject, for the national subject, for the state as failed paternal figure, and for the failures of fatherhood, which form a chain of collapsing masculinities that contribute towards a collective sense of regional orphanhood. The texts studied here stage the antagonisms of gender, sexuality and nation through deconstructions of the family, hegemonic masculinity, motherhood, revolutionary romanticism and the relationship of humans with animals. Elements of horror are often introduced, but blended in a new way to produce fiction with psychological and moral resonance. Signs of distress abound as the literature explores issues of urban alienation, emptiness, isolation, the loss of self, the nature of love and despair, vulnerability and the constant fear of violence, but also occasional moments of beauty; disaffected from the prevailing social, political and cultural norms, characters often retreat into inner exile and fantasy. The style of these narratives often allows no anchorage as small harmonies are uprooted and mutilated on the next page. Flashes of hope soar momentarily only to fall back and wilt. The use of space and time is indicative of the difficult historical moment in which these authors write — a moment of compressed, claustrophobic space and stagnation of time, immobility, a special kind of tragedy. A generation of writers drag the past like a dead corpse and confront an uncertain and precarious present as Central Americans attempt to find their niche within neoliberal globalization.

In spite of the overall depressing image at times that issues from this fiction, and whether or not this amounts to a recognisable generational and regional mentality or affect (melancholy, mourning, cynicism, nihilism or even a sense of metaphysical orphanhood), these writers are also involved, in however a minor way, in the building of a new culture through a staging of new subjectivities and a new ethics. This is a transitional generation processing the past and the hope is that the desires they express will be requited one day. The fictional constructs discussed here also refract the everyday gender troubles we are familiar with in contexts beyond Central America. Writers are pushing back against patriarchy through fictional images of strong female agency and the deconstruction of masculinity, but also through the problematization of the figure of the mother, a taboo in the Hispanic world. Two of the female authors studied in this book, Jacinta Escudos and Denise Phé-Funchal, as well as a male author, Carlos Cortés, all join a now well-established sub-genre of Central American literature depicting castrating fictional mothers.[3]

Why contemporary Central America fiction in particular? The panorama of Spanish American fiction has long been dominated by Mexico, Argentina, Colombia, Uruguay and Chile and to a lesser extent Cuba and Peru. Central America, on the other hand, has tended to be represented either by the past (Miguel Ángel Asturias) or politicized fiction flowing out of the Central American civil wars, especially the quasi-literary form of the *testimonio* genre. Nevertheless, the region has always boasted a rich and varied fictional output, even though until the last twenty years it has never really pushed through into the mainstream patterns of literary consumption in Latin America, let alone the rest of the world. In fact, a long-term complaint has been the lack of distribution and take-up in Central America itself. This has all changed with the rise of new literary figures, or more accurately, the recognition of existing writers largely invisible outside Central America: alongside the authors studies in this book, there are Dante Liano, Carol Zardetto, Francisco Goldmann, Anacristina Rossi, Horacio Castellanos Moya, Tatiana Lobo, Miguel Huezo Mixco, Rafael Menjívar Ochoa (1959–2011), Ana María Rodas, Rafael Cuevas Molina, Javier Payeras, Lizandro Chávez Alfaro and Erick Blandón, to name just a few of the most prominent, but also a series of younger writers pushing through.[4] Ironically, the door had been opened by that very politicized fiction from which many writers in the last twenty years have been keen to take some distance. The growing popularity of Central American fiction with publishing houses in Spain and France is now being followed by the English-speaking world. Central American fiction is now routinely translated into other languages (albeit Western European ones) and Central American writers are regularly winning literary prizes outside the region. This mini-Boom (a term which no contemporary writer would be happy to subscribe to since the Boom of the 1960 and 1970s has been so overlaid with ideology, stereotyping and marketing), has run parallel with the formation of more local, regional publishing houses, such as the Guatemalan F&G Editores and the Costa Rican Uruk Editores, Anamá Ediciones in Nicaragua, Arcoiris in El Salvador and Guaymuras in Honduras, as well as a concomitant rise in literary-critical interest in Central American fiction around the world.[5]

But why these particular fictions and these particular writers? I have chosen these fictions either because they were recommended to me or because they chose me — they imposed themselves on me, their aesthetic imagination exercising my own imagination. This then is my affective corpus. The choices may appear idiosyncratic to others and have key omissions, omissions which the field or its hegemonic critics may demand to be included (the works of Horacio Castellanos Moya and Anacristina Rossi are a case in point). But one simply cannot include everything. I sought a representational cross-section of fictional works from different countries across the region, but most of all I only chose novels or short stories that I derived pleasure from reading. I make no apologies for my choices — when you are not in church, you don't have to worry about heresy. Nor is the corpus intended as a counter-canon, since in many ways the Nicaraguan writer Sergio Ramírez and the Guatemalan Rey Rosa have become canonic, whether they wish to see themselves that way or not. There is no gay literature or literature in Indigenous languages or Afro-descendant literature represented in my corpus. These omissions are neither deliberate nor blind, but rather obey an idiosyncratic choice of texts which I happened upon by accident or were recommended to me or which were simply the ones I could access or which caught my critical eye for some reason or another and compelled me to engage with them. And rather than make value judgments of the type — are the fictions analyzed good or bad? — I lean more towards Foucault's call for 'a kind of criticism that would try not to judge but to bring an oeuvre, a book, a sentence, an idea to life'.[6] For some writer's I analyse just one of their novels (Ruiz Puga, Ramírez, Galich, Cortés), one book of short stories (Halfon, Hernández) or indeed just one single short story (Rey Rosa). For others I range over more than one work (Phé-Funchal, Escudos). My intention is less to give an encompassing analysis of a writer's complete oeuvre than engage with the philosophical, ethical or artistic ideas that have caught my attention in their writings. All these Central American authors, as well as numerous others, deserve their own book-length scholarly studies. It is hoped that this challenge will be taken up by other literary critics sooner rather than later.

Along with this surge of literary creativity and its enthusiastic reception has also come a shift in the field of Central American literary criticism. Philosophical and psychoanalytic readings now sit side by side with political ones. Every theory that is common currency in the North Atlantic nations, from poststructuralism in its many guises (Derrida, Foucault, Deleuze, Butler, Kristeva, Barthes, Baudrillard), to postcolonial critique, European philosophy from Hegel to Heidegger, Benjamin to Bauman, feminism and queer theory, Lacanian psychoanalysis and the cultural materialism of Williams and Hall, all are handled with aplomb by self-confident critics both inside and outside Central America working on this fiction. Critics are also adept at applying Latin America's homegrown 'decolonial' critique, as well as the continuing relevance of Marxist and sociological approaches to criticism. This growing sophistication has also led to a re-appraisal of what literature stands for — the epistemological status of the literary and its relationship to politics. Here, I need to state my position in no uncertain terms. While I acknowledge that the subjectivities on display in the novels discussed are determined, at least in part, by the civil wars and violence, they cannot be reduced to simplistic notions of social denunciation. They do not neatly fit a determinist model. Nor can they be held to demands for political compromise or ethical obligations to this or that programmatic agenda. Some progressive literary criticism is still too attached to a kind of literary realism masquerading as truth. However, as Frederic Jameson reminds us: 'If it is social truth or knowledge we want from realism, we will soon find that what we get is ideology' (Jameson 2015: 6). Ever since at least the days of nineteenth-century republican romanticism and Latin American *modernismo*, Latin American literary criticism in general has been dogged by the idea that literature intervenes significantly in the formation of citizen subjectivity such that in times of conflict and social change literature should play a role in propagating revolutionary messages or positive images of the present or the future; that is to say, literature is saddled with a didactic, statist function. But literature, like art in general, has no such pedagogical or exemplary obligation — the artist as embodiment of the social collective.

In most contemporary Central American fiction there is more often than not no plot resolution linking back into some primal unity, which might reunite the conflictive multiplicity of events, no comforting or satisfying denouement that might lead the reader to think all is finally right with this fictional world, no exemplary instance of good winning out against evil. Closure, as distinct from mere ending or conclusion, suggests a resolution to the tension driving the narrative, but in much Central American contemporary fiction endings are deliberately unresolved — Arcadia, Escudo's disenchanted protagonist, the fictions of Rey Rosa notoriously so, the suicide of Ana in Phé Funchal's *Ana sonríe*, which provides a death but no closure (the conditions that produced her decision to end her life persist), the flight towards oblivion at the end of Ramírez's *Margarita*, the boy staring out the window at the end of Halfon's 'Death of a Catcher', and so forth. And this lack of closure has indirect political resonance: it gestures towards the many unresolved tensions in post-civil war Central American daily life. Central American fiction is thus a transformational space for processing differing individual and social traumas, the legacies of two hundred years of colonialism as much as the civil wars of the 1970s and 80s. The fact that no happy endings are provided should not concern us and should not be seen as 'post-politics'. In addition, it depends on what we mean by 'politics'. The disenchantment apparent in Central American fiction is palpable in the literary critics. Literary criticism joins a chorus of denunciation of social injustice and it does so by highlighting and ventriloquising the overt political content of Central American fiction in an act of regional solidarity. In many ways this is highly appropriate and logical. But even though some of it provides insightful analysis leading to new positions, new knowledge, some of it would seem to use the fiction as merely a vehicle for stating political positions, underplaying the verbal artistry. Both socially committed literature and its attendant criticism, while not showing an aversion to affect and interiority, prefer to focus attention on the more abstract political-economic forces that shape our lives and often risk coming across as preachy and propagandistic (I run the same risk myself). The best of Central American post-war criticism, however, works in the space between both, denying neither dimension. I will return to this point shortly when I consider the work of Jacques Rancière and how it might inform our approach to aesthetics and politics and, by extension, our approach to literary criticism. For now, let me state that writers should write whatever they want without feeling obligations of any kind or prescription, save that of writing well.

Alexandra Ortiz Wallner and Beatriz Cortez are key referents in contemporary debates on Central America fiction and have published book-length studies. Ortiz Wallner's corpus in *El arte de ficcionar: la novela contemporánea en Centroamérica* (2012), like

Cortez's *Estética del cinismo*, extends from the 1980s to 2006 and like Cortez and most Central American literary critics (myself included), the civil war and post-civil war period is the inescapable referent. If we approach Central America in a geographical mode, it is more than an additive unity of separate localisms lacking in any over-arching organic unity, save that of regional climate. It is an organic, though diverse, social and cultural unity constantly under threat of obliteration by the disaggregating forces of capitalist globalisation and with a common memory of colonisation. I take my description of Central America from Ortiz, who conceptualises it thus:

> a cultural-linguistic-literary region that includes seven national states: Belize, Guatemala, El Salvador, Honduras, Nicaragua, Costa Rica and Panama. [...] Given its condition of a space of constant transit, both the cultural-literary productions of the physical-geographical territory and those emanating from further afield of these national and regional frontiers, are included in this conception of Central America. (Ortiz Wallner 2012: 10)

This latter point is used by Ortiz to remind us that contemporary Central American fiction writers are marked by their 'nomadism', by their 'constant displacement within and without Central America', giving rise to a 'literature without fixed residence' (11) and a decentring of nationalism as the primary referent. For her part, Guatemalan writer Denise Phé-Funchal highlights a kind of negative unity among Central American writers similarly linked to a shared, abject history and violent contemporary reality:

> Culturally, the Central America that I know is very diverse [...] The ways of feeling, of perceiving life, of love, of money, of politics , the assumption of an identity [...] are completely different. However, there is no doubt that there are things that unite us: political disorder, the indifference of the State towards the people, migration to the United States, corruption, poverty, drug traffickers, generalized violence, insecurity [...] Surely this crude reality is one of the themes that unite regional literature. (Phé-Funchal, 'Denise Phé-Funchal' n/d)

Ortiz goes on to acknowledge the foundational work on general histories of Central American fiction done by the likes of Ramón Luis Acevedo, Magda Zavala, and Arturo Arias (Acevedo: 1982; Zavala 1990; & Arias 2007). She emphasizes how Central American fiction has largely been marginalised from the reception of more general Latin American and international fiction until the last twenty years. She concludes her book by returning to her title, *El arte de ficcionar* (The Art of Doing Fiction), to re-emphasise, as my own book does, that the key is in the 'art' and not the ability to faithfully mimic political or historical reality. However, it is impossible to neatly separate literature from politics, so how we actually conceptualize their relationship is crucial, lest we mouth clichés about politics or sociologize literature out of business. Jacques Rancière can help us to understand what is at stake.

Though the literary-critical wars between different schools of criticism have largely subsided, there is still an unspoken division between those who pursue political and sociological ideology critique so as to celebrate or indict texts according to whether or not they display a progressive ideology, and those who, while not denying the political and historical entanglements of literary texts, nevertheless wish to also explain how a work of art functions *as art*. If politics is considered a form of rational persuasion for political ends, then literary aesthetics is an uneasy partner. Another way of saying this is to declare that a literary text is not exhausted by sociology critique. In fact its true political import might be in the way it opens up a space of thinking not bracketed by fidelity to some known historical record or doctrinaire set of political values, a space in which invention and chance connections can provide alternative configurations of what can be thought, heard, said and done. The supposed clash between artistic and political values, which has regularly come to the fore in Latin American literature and criticism, especially during times of dictatorship, revolution and the Cold War, is a false one. Is art's primary function ethico-political or artistic? Who shall decide and with what warrant? Art that turns away from nation building or political compromise is often dismissed as an evasion, as a dilettante exercise, an example of art for art's sake. But such an accusation highlights a lingering conception of literature that still haunts a lot of Latin American literary criticism: literature as primarily a statist, and thus political, practice. The issue is not about abandoning politics, however, but about critiquing critical stances that reduce literature to a purely ideologizing function. In *The Politics of Aesthetics*, Rancière declares: 'Commitment is not a category of art. That does not mean that art is apolitical. It means that aesthetics has its own politics, or its own meta-politics'; 'there are no criteria for establishing a correspondence between aesthetic virtue and political virtue' (Rancière 2006: 60; 61). Rancière prefers to speak about what he terms 'the distribution of the sensible' (*le partage du sensible*), a kind of unwritten law, as the true target of politics in aesthetics. It governs:

> the sensible order that divides places and forms of participation in a common world by first establishing the modes of perception within which they are inscribed. The distribution of the sensible thus produces a system of self-evident perceptual facts based on the horizons and fixed modalities of what is visible and audible as well as what can be said, thought or done. Strictly speaking, then, 'distribution' refers to both forms of inclusion and exclusion. (85)

According to Rancière, art can describe experiences which can destabilise the system of normative divisions that defines the relations between things in the common world; that is, the organization of conditions that limit what one can see, hear and say. This is what Rancière describes as '*dissensus*' and the politics of the aesthetic. Dissensus is the process of transforming the given world, 'the sensible', by putting it in conflict with a dissenting, rival, or otherwise contrary conception of the world. For Joseph Tanke, Rancière's *dissensus* means 'the development of the unexpected, what has no script, the unidentified [...] Art operates on objects, distinctions and borders of the sensitive, helping expand what can be seen and heard [...] offers alternative temporalities and spaces, and calls into question how the sensible configuration of the world is presented to us and given to us' (Tanke 2011: 105). For Rancière, then, the rupture that art can offer, as a political act, is expressed as the dissensus that creates fissures in the established order of the sensible and gives birth to 'a new political subject' (Rancière 2006: 85).

And it is, in fact, a new 'political subject' that can be detected in the general contours of contemporary Central American fiction, which taken as a whole is involved in a kind of collective 'clearing out' — everything is up for redistribution and *dissensus*, in Rancière's terms: deconstruction of the institution of the family, hegemonic masculinity, motherhood, revolutionary romanticism, and the relationship of humans with animals, all themes in this book. Multiple deconstructions have cleared the way for new subjectivities to emerge. These new subjectivities begin to appear largely after the Central American peace accords, after the electoral loss of the Sandinistas, and during the onset of what is loosely called economic and cultural globalisation. Novels of the last twenty-five years present new kinds of subjectivity submerged or absent during the phase of 'heroic witnessing' in *testimonio* writing or revolutionary poetry. But there is no hope for a utopian plenitude of the subject in contemporary Central American fiction, just a staging of unresolved conflict, including with subjectivity itself as an effect of alienation. Though that alienation may come from the historical context in which it has been produced, we cannot subordinate these literary texts in historicist fashion to their socio-historical contexts, as mere 'symptoms of their cultures'. For Todd McGowan: 'literary texts are primarily valuable not for (nor simply reducible to) what they reveal about their cultural contexts, but rather for how they break from their contexts in order to articulate what a culture cannot directly articulate about itself' (McGowan 2017: 92).

Needless to say, this new political subject calls forth a necessary new criticism.In one sense literary criticism is like literature itself: a movement towards new significations, new discursive links, new logics of social relations, a disruption of the 'normal' distribution of sense, including 'commonsense'. Literary language can provide a new relation of a given subject to the Symbolic, a different constellation of symbolizations of the antagonisms of life. Aesthetics, as a mode of de-identification, gives us the possibility of getting out of ourselves a little, of being led to undetermined areas, without such fixed coordinates, to be moved and often challenged. Our imagination released from its routine perceptions. One would think, then, that the only way to be properly faithful to a creative artistic work is surely to undertake a creative re-writing —sticking to the supposed authorial intentions or the *fábula* on the surface of the text or reducing the text to a doctrinaire political position is the safest way to betray the spirit of the original. Literature resists literary criticism because it resonates beyond its conditions of production. The only way to keep a work alive and re-signifying is to leave it 'open', future-oriented, so it goes on releasing interpretive potential. If a fictional text deals with the 'could have been', rather than a faithful reproduction of a factual reality, then should not literary criticism, criticism worthy of the name, also respond to the same creative urge and provide a creative dialogue with the original to produce new ideas, to create new connections? We must attune ourselves to other conversations, including our own with ourselves — our own experiences and desires reanimated in the reading process: 'look up often, to listen to something else', Barthes says. Not to do so closes off the great (Barthesian) pleasures in reading. Our literary criticism must be open to this creative reanimation, allowing our own desire to have free rein — an erotics of reading. What we have therefore are two interrelated processes of subjectivization revealed through acts of self-disclosure in writing: one through the author and one through the reader-critic who writes a response — reading as the performance of self vicariously through the reception of fictional characters. Literary criticism produces a creative re-assemblage of a literary text's elements within an explicative narrative, which, though it has analytical and objectivist intentions, is nonetheless a creative, rhetorical re-emplotment of a literary text's being.

These novels and short stories are therefore more about the emotional and the psychological: they represent the affective experience of domestic and societal violence, parental separation, sexual and amorous disappointment, preoccupation with love, grief, childhood, and the loss of faith in societal mores and political utopias. They express and represent not the facts of history (autobiographical or otherwise) but the affective and physical conditions of mind and body *in* history and their influence on subjectivity. It is not a question of historical accuracy in fiction, but rather of the impressions that past events and their memory have imprinted on both the authors and their fictional creations: narrative fiction as the attempt by an authorial subjectivity to summon a readership around it through affect as much as story-telling, since the two are inextricably intertwined. Beyond the powers of story-telling unfolding in the fictions studied here, it is often the affect generated which keeps the reader reading: the palpable joy in Ruiz Puga's *Got seif de Cuin!*, Ramírez's *Margarita está linda la mar* leavened by implicit bitterness for the course *sandinismo* took, the visceral and acid tone in Galich's fallen angels, Escudos's disenchanted women, the ethico-aesthetic dimension opened up through affective encounters with animals in Claudia Hernández's 'Carretera sin buey' and Rey Rosa's 'Gracia', the neo-existentialist solitude of Halfon's narrator as his childhood idyll crumbles, the disappointment of Phé Funchal's women, and Carlos Cortés's brooding atmosphere of regret and loathing. These fictions offer an understanding of the way in which violence functions affectively, as something that allows for fantasy and reality to be mixed so as to produce not only an emotional response of empathy or antipathy, but a philosophical-ethical response — not moral didacticism, but rather an aesthetic staging of a possible world which impels us to be active readers and make a hypothetical choice, a sovereign decision — where do we stand on the matters raised in these fictions? Affect, then, is not meaning as such, but rather a catalyst to bodily reaction and vice versa. It can only be identified or registered in the traces it leaves in our emotions and actions as these come to consciousness and are expressed in language. How the reader perceives it is dependent upon his or her own attunement to the rhythms of affect often disregarded or neglected when the reading process is focused primarily on some overt expression of content or narrative action. The affect released in the reading process activates the body and the body talks. The nexus between the writing and reading bodies, texts and experience, 'operationalizes' affect, activates its potential. Its effects, however, are never predictable. These fictions may not impel us to take to the streets, no matter how much their context is the tragedies of Central American politics and history, but they reward us with a more intimate wisdom — the ability to tell a story that moves us.

The first three chapters of this book deal with national longing, belonging or 'dis-belonging', aesthetic attempts to exorcize not only violent national pasts shot through with colonialism and dictatorship, but also a certain kind of heroic, masculine revolutionary subjectivity that became a hegemonic ideologeme for the Left. Here, affect is nomadic, looking for a new object of attachment in the wake of the collapse of both the national subject and the revolutionary subject. Each of the three novels studied — David Ruiz Puga's *Got seif de Cuin!*, Sergio Ramírez's *Margarita, está linda la mar*, and Franz Galich's *Managua Salsa City*— seeks its own way through the thicket of history. Chapters 4, 5 & 6 look at the figuration of the paternal in Rodrigo Rey Rosa's short story 'Gracia', Eduardo Halfon's *Mañana nunca lo hablamos*, and Carlos Cortés' *Larga noche hacia mi madre*. 'Gracia' is a coded indictment of the violence of patriarchal Judeo-Christian sacrifice and the question of our relation to non-human animals; Halfon's stories explore the loss of a childhood idyll and the racial and class divides in Guatemalan society, depicted in the narrator's family's class privilege in the context of an authoritarian, masculine state; and Carlos Cortés's novel throws into relief the failed masculinities of an extended family and their effects on women. Chapters 7, 8 & 9 deal with themes of the body — dead bodies, gendered bodies, sexualized bodies and suicidal bodies — as well as masculinity and violence, a common theme throughout the book. Chapter 7 looks at the animalization of human bodies in Claudia Hernández's short stories in the context of El Salvador's civil violence, but also, as in Rey Rosa's short story, the re-imagining of animals as moral subjects; Chapter 8 reads Jacinta Escudos' melancholy female protagonists and their bodily drives against the background of unreconstructed masculinity. This theme is continued in Denise Phé-Funchal's fiction, in which women struggle against societal gender roles, leading to tragic outcomes. A violent tear in the symbolic fabric of being and conviviality haunts all these fictions. It calls forth an act of suture or restitution, but the lost object can never be restored (the mutilated body, the failed revolution, the dead father, the absent partner, childhood innocence). It can only be compensated for and worked through. Literary art can help in that work of mourning.

A note on translations

All translations from the Spanish originals, whether from the fictional works or from the works of other critics, are my own.

PART I

Exorcizing the
National/Revolutionary Subject

1

With Crystalline Drops of Imperial Jade

David Ruiz Puga's *Got seif de Cuin!*

'Strange whim of the people! They demand their history from the hand of the poet and not from the hand of the historian.'

HEINRICH HEINE[7]

DAVID RUIZ PUGA (1966–) is a Belizean writer and educator of Mayan descent born in Benque Viejo del Carmen. He has published several books, including the short story collections *Old Benque* (1990), *La Visita* (2000), the bilingual *Jonás Matapalo* (2002) for children and *Under the Yax'ché Tree: On Legends, Tales and Apparitions in Western Belize* (2010). His only novel is *Got Seif De Cuin!*(1995), which has won him wider recognition in Central America and abroad.

British Honduras, the official name of Belize until 1973, was always a bit of a no-man's land for Europeans, even after the Spanish Crown had formally claimed it as its own. Eighteenth-century British and Scottish pirates, the legendary 'Baymen', settled there and were instrumental in the hardwood logging industry along the Belize River and the introduction of African slaves. An uneasy accommodation was established with both the Spanish Crown and subsequent British Government as the terri-tory gradually became a British protectorate after the Spanish

17

granted occupation rights to the settlers in exchange for repelling piracy. Its history has produced a mixed-race and multi-ethnic society with a variety of languages spoken, including English (the official national language), Creole English (Kriol), Spanish (recognized as an official sub-language), the transnational Garifuna (an African-Indigenous language derived mostly from Arawak and spoken in several Central American countries' coastal communities), and Mayan Indigenous languages (Kekchi, Mopan, Yucatec), though it is recognized that most Belizeans are tri-lingual in Spanish, English Kriol and Mayan languages; all this in a country with a current population estimated at only 380,000.

Belize has never been considered a fully authentic part of the dominant Spanish-speaking Central American nations because of its official language, English, and because it never achieved independence, like the ex-Spanish colonies of the region, until fully 150 years later. Its coastline faces towards the Caribbean, which has shaped its history as much as the terrestrial Mayan civilization. It has thus suffered historically from a double marginalization: as part of Central America, it is considered part of a region stereotyped as a collection of unredeemable, mono-cultural 'banana republics' with tin-pot dictators; and because of the strong presence of a mixed ex-slave population and thus its dual identity as both *mestizo* and black Anglo-Caribbean (Creole and Garifuna) it does not fit the dominant perception of a fellow Central American *mestizo* nation. Until independence in the 1980s, Belizean Creoles, originally a mixed union of ex-African slaves, polyglot buccaneers and Europeans, were a moderate majority of the Belizean population. They have thus tended to be seen as representative of Belizean national identity, even though significant numbers have migrated to the United States since then and there has been a parallel influx of *mestizo* Central Americans, such that the Creoles are considered to make up a third or less of the current population. People deemed Mayan by the official census make up some 12 per cent of the population and predominantly represent three different Indigenous groups. The double marginalization of Belize is thus further complicated externally by Guatemala's continued territorial claim over the land.[8] Internally, the Spanish-speaking people of Indigenous descent have traditionally had a subordinate status reflected, among other things, in the national literary canon dominated by English-language writers.[9] It is against the backdrop of this complex national linguistic-ethnic mix that Ruiz Puga locates his Indigenous-*mestizo* heritage and his novel.

Published in 1995, *Got seif de Cuin!* is a short novella in Spanish written in a predominantly English-speaking country. It is no surprise that *Got Seif de Cuin!* was first published in Guatemala. It is a delightful little masterpiece of scarcely 78 pages and the author's enjoyment in writing it is evident. With a deceptively simple language tinged with folklore, it recounts the fictional history of an unnamed Spanish-speaking village of Mayan descent in the Río Viejo (Belize River) region of what we recognize today as Belize, though the name Belize is never used in the novel. Though there are brief references to the time when Río Viejo was under Spanish colonial rule until the loss of the Central American colonies, most of the narrative is taken up with the period when Belize was known as the colony of British Honduras from 1862, until its subsequent granting of self-governance by Great Britain in 1964 and the recognition of formal independence as a nation-state in 1981.

The novel begins with Don Enrique, the mayor of the town, on his death bed. The narrator, from within the popular consciousness of the community, relates the village's enchanted origins through the old man's consciousness:

> When Don Enrique, the last mayor directly named by her Majesty, lay dying in his bed, he noticed that the village where he had lived for 100 years had no name. It was known as the end of the world in the enchanted region of the Tipú, in a corner of Río Viejo. The morning when Catarina D'Aragón wetted his tongue with a piece of canvas soaked in water, the spirit of he who loved his village until death began to wander through time . . .
>
> One sombre grey day when the clouds hung heavy over the noggins of the people, there arrived in the village a blue-eyed priest with a turned-up nose who had come to establish a school in order to teach everyone the language in which Her Majesty wished her subjects to communicate. (Ruiz Puga 1995: 9)

Thus Río Viejo passed under the control of the British Crown, an event presaged in a vision that came to Don Enrique in which Río Viejo would henceforth be the site of a struggle for territorial control between Fayabón (Guatemala) and England.

Colonisation by the British also signalled the loss of prestige of the village's elder and spiritual leader, don Justo, the last reported link by birth to the Mayan Tipú tribe:

> Don Justo had been the only mayor for many, many years. Everyone knew he was the only survivor of the mystical city of the Tipú, lost in time, where the corn cobs grew with grains of gold and where Chaac came down to water the crops with crystalline drops of imperial jade. (12)

Told from the perspective of the Spanish-speaking Belizeans of Mayan descent, the story proceeds to aesthetically recover a submerged history and highlights the problems of a people and a town marginalized in the course of the key historical events, yet which is nevertheless impacted by the same series of political changes and revolts through one hundred and fifty years of colonial domination. *Got seif de Cuin!* is clearly situated within the dynamics of the nationalist movement in its fictional and humorous retelling of history. We can cite Ruiz Puga himself on this in 'Panorama del texto literario en Belice, de tiempos coloniales a tiempos post-coloniales', in which he refers to this movement as 'the cultural policy of the new multi-ethnic society' (Ruiz Puga 2001: 3). This may be so, but we are still faced with a fictional novel and not mimetic History, however much the novel re-models real referents. Though the historical context of the novel's events is the hegemonic power of Great Britain, which has promoted ethnic amnesia, what one can extract from the novel's reading, I would suggest, is less a thinly veiled aesthetic version of Belizean national history than an imaginative construction of the affective popular consciousness of a geographical and cultural sub-section of a Central American nation buffeted by historical change, a portrayal recognisable in other ethnic or oppressed minorities in the region. The result is not too distant from two classics of twentieth-century Latin American literature, intertextually referenced on more than one occasion: Gabriel García Márquez's *Cien años de soledad* (One Hundred Years of Solitude) and Juan Rulfo's canonical *Pedro Páramo*.[10] While the echoes of Gabriel García Márquez's *One Hundred Years of Solitude* are unmistakeable, we are in different territory, geographically and culturally, and there will be no apocalyptic denouement with a biblical hurricane destroying all traces of the village, no pessimistic view of history, no tragic vision. Instead we have the aesthetic redemption of a people caught in colonial transition, surviving with what tools they have at hand, weapons of the underdog: cultural tradition, resilience, dialects that bind, solidarity, humour and faith in the future. The trajectory is upward to liberation and independence. This turn to the affective and to the popular (language and spontaneity), and 'intranscendence' — the rejection of metaphysical concerns (save the occasional references to Indigenous cosmology and myth) in favour of a perspective from within and for the popular classes — involves the vernacular as a source of both popular identity and popular myth-making, expressed by an insider, as it were, who knows and feels the daily rhythms of rural life, who writes in an unpretentious, yet profound way — no modernist technical innovations here.

Ruiz Puga gives a sense of the historical past as a compound of fragmented knowledges, especially those of personal, family and tribal memory. Whereas in *One Hundred Years* we witness the ascent and then the fall of an idealistic community with a movement reminiscent from Genesis to Eden and then to Apocalypse, *Got seif de Cuin!* narrates a less grandiose trajectory: a slow and triumphant ascent and the movement from a mystical, legendary past (the memories of the Mayan indigenous descendants of the region) to a sober modernity. And this says a lot about the historical balance in Belize after independence, compared to other countries like Colombia (or Nicaragua, the setting of Sergio Ramírez's *Margarita, está linda la mar*, discussed in Chapter 2). There are several key moments of transition in the novel: the British displacement of the Spanish and the taking of administrative control of the town; the succession of British monarchs registered in the changing of portraits in the town hall; the rise of the independence movement symbolized by 'the man with the tropical shirt' (the people of the town opt for a revolutionary movement of independence, but one of decidedly peaceful, anti-militarist resistance); the arrival of President Carvajal and the political intrigue as he tries to claim Río Viejo for Fayabón; and the eventual granting of self-governance to the colony, returning the narrative to its beginning with Don Enrique on his death bed. All these events amount to outside influences intruding on a settled way of life.

References to Queen Victoria locate the novel's beginning in the mid-nineteenth century, when Río Viejo became a British colony. The novel registers, with strong doses of humour, the astonishment of the people of the town before the changes of political leaders and national borders, apparently without reason. The dying Don Enrique remembers a gray and gloomy day when a British priest 'with blue eyes and a snub nose' arrived in the village to establish a school to teach 'the language in which His Majesty wanted His subjects to communicate', signalling the Babelic confusion of tongues the villagers would be required to endure throughout their history as successive colonial overlords shaped their destiny:

> When Don Enrique, the Prioste of the Church, asked the priest what monarch he was referring to, he responded with anger that he spoke no less than of Sovereign Queen Victoria, Empress of India. Everyone gasped.
>
> 'We're screwed! They already sold us to India!' Don Enrique clenched his jaws and walked in thought toward the church of guano to take down the portrait of the King of Spain. He was the only one who claimed to know what the world was, for he possessed the only map, drawn many years ago, by a gigantic white man who had come, mounted on a black beast, to bring civilization on behalf of His Majesty, absolute lord of New Spain. (Ruiz Puga 1995: 9)

While the villagers knelt to receive the blessing of the priest, 'they glanced up at the missionary's nose, which pointed upward like a thumb. But they all refused to speak the new language. The truth was that they got tongue-tied, as happened when people came from far away saying that they had blood lines to the nobility of the kingdoms of Iberia' (10). The situation only got worse when subsequently the sub-nosed white priest, brought German nuns to teach at his school:

> My mother tells me that her grandfather told her that her father said that at the time, such a confusion arose that the children came out speaking 'Ispamal'— a mixture of English, Spanish, Mayan Yucatec and German; sufficient reason for that Governor who had the courage to visit the town to write in the annals of the   colony:

I have heard German nuns trying to teach Mayan children from a book written in English that they had to explain in Spanish . . . .

Thus the town became isolated more and more from the rest of the world. (10)

The fragment presents in microcosm the political-cultural situation that comes to complicate the life of the people throughout its history. *Got seif de Cuin!* could well serve as a thesis on interculturality since, if we separate out, just for a moment, the skeleton of the fictional context, we have a contact zone of quite distinct cultures and languages (not exactly the stereotypical 'melting pot'), in which situations that arise require negotiation in terms of both body language, linguistic register and cultural display (the juxtaposition of objects and dress identifying cultures as different); a veritable intercultural laboratory, a fictional scenario perhaps unparalleled in Central American fiction.

The stupefaction of the townsfolk at the arrival of outsiders is based as much on linguistic, as political and cultural shock. In 'Precious Water, Priceless Words: Fluidity and Mayan Experience on the Guatemalan-Belizean Border', Jennifer Gómez foregrounds the historical plight of Belize's Indigenous populations and concentrates on 'code-switching and multilingualism as techniques of resistance' (Gómez 2016: 23). She appeals to the metaphor of fluidity to describe the way people of Mayan descent have learned to negotiate historical change through linguistic flexibility and adherence to Mayan 'epistemologies of water that enable the community to survive and thrive' (23). The river, in this sense, is supremely important, linked to Mayan cosmology in scared origins. Río Viejo had merely traversed what was a common territory from before colonial times, uniting Indigenous people, whose belonging did not obey national boundaries. A common area of commerce and communication, indeed blood ties, which united rather than divided and brought mutual benefits to all, would henceforth be marked by the river into separate legal demarcations, signalled by Don Enrique nailing a humorous sign next to the river: 'Here English territory ends and the territory of shotguns begins'. Reference is also made to maps throughout and as we know, maps are also cultural weapons, symbolic representations that, like the trappings of colonial government lampooned in references to uniforms, portraits and objects symbolising power, give a concrete visualization of empire that helps to centre the consciousness of 'subjects'.

Change and difference is also registered through physical differences. Ruiz Puga uses epithetical description, reminiscent of Homeric style: 'the general with the solid body', 'the man with the monocle', 'the gentleman in the *guayabera* shirt', 'the officials with bodies of bulls', 'the gentleman with glasses', 'the bald man with the body of a trunk', 'the black man with honey-coloured eyes', 'the man with the penetrating eyes and manicured moustache', 'the man with the upturned nose', etc. Those outside the community are referenced by physical traits, even when their political or administrative function and their names have previously been mentioned, symbolizing their outsider-ness and presenting them as the townspeople first see them in all their incongruity. This situates focalization inside the community at the level of popular consciousness. At one stage the narrator makes a locative reference focalized through don Enrique, as if it were stream of consciousness, during a night of curfew when he steals across the river: 'One of those nights, Don Enrique appeared on the edge of the river with a bag on his back [propaganda for the resistance]. He had hidden for hours in a bushy area near Doña Elvira's beach' (Ruiz Puga 1995: 41). Who is Doña Elvira? We are not told. But if you belonged to the town you would know. This knowing pitch to the local extends to stylized speech patterns and rhetorical devices, like rural popular simile: their jaws trembled 'like marbles in a rag bag'; the cold made 'their ankles knock together like corn grains in maracas'; the old man's head 'felt large and heavy like a green gourd'; Don Enrique's pride 'melted like the black wax used for making candles on the Day of Dead'.

After the death of the old mayor, Don Justo, Don Enrique becomes the new mayor of the town, in fact the last to be invested in the name of the Queen of England. Another comic situation arises when Don Felipe hears that a representative of the British Crown ('the white man, He of the upturned nose') will be making a visit to the town, he summons the town folk to explain the reception that has been devised and how the townsfolk should dress themselves and their houses and follow a set instruction for the parade. One can only imagine the stentorian, affected oratorical style of Don Enrique attempting to assert his authority over the village. But he has a final point:

'Ah! I almost forgot . . . ', continued the old man stretching is scrawny neck: 'I inform you that Don Felipe has changed the name of his marimba . . . it's is now called The Brittanica and it will be the marimba that plays the welcome piece, *Ave Lira* . . . So then, whoever gets caught calling Don Felipe's marimba Spanish Echoes, will have to face the consequences!' People were left perplexed. Don Enrique cast his gaze over the entire towns- people and shrugging his shoulders barked out: 'Don't even think of it . . . The law demands it . . . God Save the Queen!' That said, the old man turned around and went into the town hall. Between murmurs about God giving wings to scorpions, the people dispersed to work out what they would do with their mud brick shacks to change their appearance for the man with the glass eye. (14)

Here we have a complex vignette: a changing of the colonial guard from Spanish to English registered through the changing name of instruments, a typical rural village welcoming event for a visiting dignitary (synecdochically reduced to the monocled eye of colonialism), a mimicking of colloquial speech, and a self-mocking joke by a narrator at the level of the fictive community he describes. Orality is not only present in the mimicking of collo-quial speech patterns, but in the very rhythm of Ruiz Puga's sentences. The narrative focalization is from within a community by one of its members. But while the narrator has a joke at Don Felipe's expense, the humour is not satirical per se (reserved for the colonial hierarchy), just teasing, typical of a society in which social hierarchy is mildly debunked to keep everyone grounded. This is a community that can laugh at itself, a subversive laugh, a community where everyone knows everyone else, where first names suffice, where a generalized feeling of belonging is never in dispute, a secular *retablo*.

By late afternoon the white representative of the Queen had not arrived. We are led to a transitional moment in the story:

Don Enrique didn't notice that the marimba had stopped playing. The old man had gone round and round thinking about how he had turned into the town's laughingstock, when suddenly, he lifted his gaze and saw that the few people still beside him were frozen still, with their jaws dropped, looking upwards. Don Enrique turned his eyes and found himself face to face with a gigantic horse, on which was a man as black as charcoal and immense, like the huge dolls in the festival of the Virgin. He sat rigid on the horse, such that as the light of the sun struck him he seemed a blue-green colour. The mayor with the curved beak felt the saliva slide down his gullet upon seeing such a man in a white military uniform. He gave a nervous croak trying to say something to unfreeze the atmosphere. He took a couple of steps back and directing a polite gaze towards the black man with white gloves, bowed and said: 'Long Live Africa!'. (16)

Ruiz Puga has a keen ear for writing prose, for the cadence of a paragraph, most likely imbibed from an oral story-telling culture, deceptively non-showy, but with a complex affective and cinematic style. The British Crown has sent its middle administrative strata to oversee the town. The image of the black man with white gloves on the horse is reminiscent of Roland Barthes' essay in *Mythologies* on the photo of a black child in uniform saluting the French flag on the cover of a 1955 *Paris Match*, a symbol of the colonies incorporated into empire[11] and only a year after the commencement of the Algerian War of Independence. The intertextuality and connotative force are unavoidable. In Ruiz Puga's cinematic set piece, a miniature, descriptive-affective marvel, the tension in the bodies, the mouths open in astonishment, the glances eager to know the outcome, and the incongruity for the Indigenous-*mestizo* townspeople of seeing a black man in white uniform and white gloves astride a big horse, also speak to incorporation into empire. The description is symbolic castration of the colonial officials through satirical portrayal. The image joins other symbols of colonial power — royal portraits, smoking jackets, edicts, flags, loyal colours, and so forth— all standing in place of a distant and inaccessible authority, to whom petitioning is nigh on impossible. It is only because the town has been drawn into border disputes between Fayabón and the British Empire that the villages strategic positioning on the river frontier, and thus their loyalty, becomes important.

I turn here to Jennifer Gómez's claim in her doctoral dissertation, Liminal Citizenry, that in Ruiz Puga's 'blackness is posited a metaphorical and a tangible threat to the indigenous subject: the first novel [Miguel Angel Asturias's *Mulata de tal*] works with blackness as a coefficient of monstrosity while the second novel

[*Got seif de Cuin!*] crafts it as a destabilizing factor' (Gómez 2011: 162). She raises an interesting issue and we need to give an account — the presence and function of mulattoes and blacks in Ruiz Puga's novel certainly warrants discussion. Some blacks and mulattoes were incorporated into the British administrative structure after the abolition of slavery, and thus functioned as extensions of the apparatus of colonial control. It is at that level that they are depicted in *Got seif de Cuin!* Gómez goes on to state: 'For Belize to claim a place in the Central American tradition, it must hinge its cultural narrative on a Spanish speaking indigenous minority along the border and not on its Anglophone black population', 162) This may have been the case 20 odd years ago, when *Got seif de Cuin!* was first published, or even in 2004 when Ruiz Puga was interviewed by the Salvadoran writer Jacinta Escudos, but that is a much harder claim to make in 2011, especially since much cultural work has been done to incorporate the Caribbean, black or otherwise, into regional debates (Mackenbach 2008; Mackenbach, Kraume & Müller 2012; Mackenbach 2014; Ette, Mackenbach, Müller & Ortiz Wallner 2016). But more importantly, Gómez insists on literal linkages between Ruiz Puga's novel and the historical record. However, this is a fiction. We can interrogate it for the broad contours of history it touches upon, but it is a fiction whose focalization, as Gómez herself attests, comes from within the *mestizo*-Indigenous community. It shows how they look out onto the world. It is thus not a political or historical treatise. The dominant Afro-Belizean Creoles were seen as part of the apparatus that oppressed them. Gómez draws a point-to-point correspondence (or lack of correspondence) to the historical record. Novels construct possible worlds which are coherent or plausible, but this is a different kind of truth from the truth of fact which an allegorical reading requires. Here we need to think about the different use of perspective both in the novel and in the writing of history. We are talking about different narrative structures: the godlike perspective of the omniscient narrator, the typical convention of historiography, versus narrative structures which represent the situatedness of all knowledge — here, a novel trying to re-create a perspective on history from within a fictional rural community dragged into border wars between competing empires and nations. But Gómez does make an important critical point:

The novel posits that by reclaiming a collective cultural identity, the Maya subject and her/his community reinscribe their
position in society and reclaim agency. They leave in their place
the black subaltern subject, whose dejection is that he himself
cannot speak, be heard or be spoken for. They can only mimic
the words of a ruler a world away they are left with the task of
fashioning a world in the image of Europe in the midst of the
tropics. Black creoles submit to mimicry while indigenous subjects retain the keen intellectual faculties of their Mesoamerican
ancestors. (169)

But again, to imagine Ruiz Puga neatly writing a fictional narrative of common agency into the Black Creoles sounds like the
reduction of novelistic discourse to the function of political
pamphleteering. Gómez closes out this section of her thesis
lamenting that the speeches in favour of common independence
and fraternity by the two blacks and the one mulatto revolutionaries in the novel are met with silence by the townsfolk. But this
is precisely the suspicion the novel wishes to convey. For
Indigenous people it always seems to be a changing of the guard,
so within the fictional construct they are right to be hesitant. This
is Ruiz Puga working the fictional puppets and showing different
sides of the situation. There is no narrative voice or character
mocking the impassioned speeches of the Creoles. Gómez ends
by asserting:

Although Indian, Chinese, Palestinian and German migrations
have significantly altered the socio-cultural dynamics of both
nations, the Mayan historical claim to the isthmus remains the
proverbial 'elephant in the room' . . . At the basis of the territorial
dispute is the matter of preserving the Mesoamerican imaginary
intact by keeping Testimonial Peoples shielded from the
processes that threaten to turn them into a New Peoples. It is an
opposition that has become increasingly challenged as Central
American national and regional imaginaries are fashioned anew
by the forces of globalization. (175)

Indeed, and the point is well taken. But to expect rural
Indigenous populations to suddenly adopt the perspective of
multicultural globalization and subaltern proletarian consciousness in the time in which the novelistic story occurs, however, is

unrealistic and imposes an activist political reading on an imaginative work of art.

Let us return to the scene of the arrival of the black representative of the British Crown. The situation becomes even more ridiculous when Don Enrique accompanies the black officer to the town hall, without knowing that there has been a change of monarch:

> Don Enrique was even more surprised when, at the Cabildo, the dark-skinned officer took the picture of Queen Victoria from the wooden frame and replaced it with a bald-headed man with a haughty look. The mayor scratched his head, not understanding what was happening. (19)

As he is about to give the same *viva* he had just uttered, he realises that the black-booted man in the photograph (King Edward VII) is wearing the same flag colours as Queen Victoria:

> The old man breathed a sigh of relief and, raising his staff in the air, greeted the officer, exclaiming: 'Got seif de Cuin!' The officer smiled and returned the salute to the mayor, who looked like one of the goblins that roamed the alleyways of the town, and with an authoritative voice that shook the mud walls of the Cabildo, exclaimed: 'God save the King!'. (Ruiz Puga 1995: 19–20)

There are a dizzying number of changes and political intrigues: King Edward VII dies and is replaced by Kings George V and VI as the mid-century independence movement begins to grow; there are border changes and the banning of what had historically been a tradition of free transit between Fayabón (Guatemala) and Río Viejo. Black administrators representing the Crown take control of the town's governance; a clandestine independence movement is established; there are attempts to woo the Río Viejo independence movement over to Fayabón and the recalcitrance of the British; and martial law is declared with a night time curfew. The changes leave the townspeople stunned and comically derisive, emphasizing the distance between daily life and national political events. Throughout the novel, and as the town is dragged into larger political schemes, a difference of perspectives arises between those in the town who do not want to rock the boat and those who want to join the wave of post-World War

II decolonisation and make a lunge for full independence. Those with an indigenous heritage are not accustomed to European legalisms, written contracts and private property:

> Don Enrique could not fall asleep that night. At two in the morning he was still tossing and turning in bed. He could not understand why the black man with honey-coloured eyes had said that the land was not theirs. Ever since he was old enough to reason, everyone had sowed corn or made their house of sticks wherever they felt like it. There were never any disagreements about land in the village, except when Don Felipe arrived saying that he had become absolute owner of the land by the river, trying to prove it with a document in his hand, on which a said General Pech of the Icaiché tribe had put his thumb stamp. The old man clenched his toothless jaws and remembered that day. (39)

The rest of the book consists of the inexorable movement toward independence. There are attempts to divide the revolutionary opposition and link Río Viejo to Fayabón, but despite the alienation of the notion of a modern nation-state for the people and the distance between the inter-party struggles and the day-to-day lives of the popular classes, marginalised from nationalist ambitions of the national elites, Ruiz Puga does not condemn the nationalist elite who lead the independence rebellion, since it is made quite clear that, in spite of its drawbacks, the national form at this juncture in the fictional construct seems the best option, since the past cannot be re-created, even if it still animates the present. Though there is brief mention of revolutionaries plotting independence, what is of note in Ruiz Puga's novel is the welcome absence of the kind of obsessive focus on individual revolutionary male heroes that one has come to expect in such novels about the journey to independence.

At the end of the novel, in a dream sequence, the dying Don Enrique is awakened by old Don Justo, the first mayor of the town, who urges him to get up and walk and come out to celebrate the self-government granted by the English, the first legal step towards independence. Thus, in the figure of Don Justo, the 100 years of struggle from the independence of Central America from Spain to the time when Río Viejo gets rid of the yoke of English colonialism, the novel tells the story of a people who, after a long history of colonialism, longer than most other Latin American countries, find an appropriate path for the future. The attitude towards history is positive, that of a triumphal march towards independence, although now within a plural and multi-ethnic identity. The affective journey is the opposite of García Márquez's *One Hundred years of Solitude*. What is refreshing about Ruiz Puga's depiction of colonial history is the palpable joy. While recognising the negative legacy of different colonialisms, especially for the Maya, Ruiz Puga refuses to end on a negative note, signalling that humour, as Jewish people endlessly remind us, is often one of the key strategies of the oppressed in over-coming or at least enduring collective, psychological trauma.

2

Nicaragua as a Novel
Sergio Ramirez's *Margarita, está linda la mar*

'Qué púberes canéforas te ofrenden el acanto.'
RUBÉN DARÍO

SERGIO RAMÍREZ (1942–) is a Nicaraguan writer, journalist and ex-politician who was the Vice-President of the Nicaraguan Sandinista revolutionary government from 1985 to 1990. He has published numerous novels, short stories and essays and is the winner of several prestigious literary awards and honours, including Knight of the Order of Arts and Letters (France, 1993) and the Alfaguara International Novel Prize 1998 for *Margarita, está linda la mar*. Among his most prominent novels are *¿Te dio miedo la sangre?* (1977), *Castigo Divino* (1988), *Un baile de máscaras* (1995), *Margarita, está linda la mar* (1998), *Sombras nada más* (2002), *Mil y una muertes* (2004), *El cielo llora por mí* (2008) and *Sara* (2015). He has also published a key memoir on the Sandinista revolution, *Adiós muchachos* (1999), and two important texts of cultural criticism: *Balcanes y volcanes y otros ensayos y trabajos* (1983) and *Estás en Nicaragua* (1986).

Margarita, está linda la mar is a text of transition in his work as it comes eight years after the collapse of the Sandinista revolutionary experiment with the shock 1990 electoral loss by the governing revolutionary political party. The current Sandinista government is a pale reflection of the idealistic days of the

Revolution. *Margarita's* thematics and the political and artistic questions it raises presage the 1999 *Adiós muchachos* (Goodbye, Boys) in which the author unloads on the failures of the revolution and the electoral loss, criticizes Leftist authoritarianism and points up the mistakes made by the *sandinistas* in the cultural sphere.[12] *Margarita, está linda la mar* fictionalizes two stories which loosely parallel two figures and two deaths that are central to twentieth-century Nicaraguan history and popular memory: the death through cirrhosis of the liver of the revered national poet, Rubén Darío, in 1916; and the assassination of the dictator Anastasio Somoza by the poet Rigoberto López in a workers social club in 1956. *Margarita* thus covers a period of fifty very important years in national life, but without pretending to be a faithful, quasi-history. Ramírez interweaves two separate, real-life stories in the same city, León, scene of much of Ramírez's literary writing, where he had studied law and which is also the scene of another key novel in his oeuvre, *Divino castigo* (Divine Punishment, 1988). Darío's death was notable for its macabre aftermath when his brain was removed for scientific study and preserved in formaldehyde, only to be subsequently stolen. The novel is based around two arrivals: that of Darío's triumphant return by boat on the *Pacific Mail* to Nicaragua in October 1907, after having established an international fame; and Somoza's arrival in León for a political rally in September 1956 to launch his re-election bid after 20 years of dictatorship. The narration is generated from a well-known centre of social life in León, the Casa Prío, a bar-restaurant. There is a group of conspirators, including Rigoberto López, who will eventually fire the murder weapon, who plot the assassination of Somoza. The narration develops through conversations between the characters as well as 'notes' from López's journal on the life of Darío. The novel uses a variety of narrative strategies, including a manipulative omniscient, third-person narrator who uses humour and irony and focalizes through the characters.

The novel begins with Captain Prío, owner of Casa Prío, observing the arrival of Somoza in León in 1956, only then to leap back in memory to the time he witnessed Rubén Darío arrive in 1907. Prío's focalization holds both stories together, as does a mute named Quirón, an orphaned child who gets to meet Darío and who later becomes a co-conspirator, La Caimana, a female fellow orphan in the same institution as Quirón, and Dr Debayle, who among other novelistic functions performs macabre operations to remove Darío's brain and later carries out a sex change operation on La Caimana, now a lesbian transvestite. One of Debayle's daughters is the Margarita of the novel's title, the one on whose fan Darío writes one of his famous poems, 'Margarita, está linda la mar'. Debayle's other daughter becomes Somoza's wife. As the conspiratorial group plans the assassination, we are presented with a dizzying kaleidoscope of sub-plots and minor events, including affairs, betrayals, military rivalries and so forth, which symbolize the chaotic nature of some of Nicaragua's history and how history is conceived in popular memory, as much as anything else, but it also make following the story a challenge at times. The complexity of the novel also points as much to the incestuous nature of life in León and the interconnection of just about everyone and everything in such a small country, whose fame as a theatre of struggle during the Cold War belies its small size.

In *Margarita* we are presented with a problematic national history not too dissimilar to *Got seif de Cuin!*, with a legacy of colonialism and foreign interventionism. But while Ruiz Puga's novel deals with the idea of a nationalism traversed by multiple cultural perspectives, its territorial integrity at stake in a struggle between an empire and an expansionist neighbour, the historical-political backdrop to *Margarita* is the struggle to liberate Nicaragua from the legacy of US regional hegemony manifest in one of its puppets, the dictator Somoza. In that sense it could be said to join a tradition of anti-imperialist Central American literature, though without the social realist didacticism. In this and other ways *Margarita* is a sort of novel of the Boom, but with a thirty-year delay: literary projections of Latin America's failure to enter Western modernity on European terms via the mimicking of a European version of nation-state formation against a backdrop of colonialism. But at the same time the novel is situated in the so-called 'post-boom', a vague and somewhat inadequate term, but which nevertheless registers the distance marked from the 'heroic' phase of the Leftist nationalism of the 1960s and 70s. It could also be said that it is a very male novel: the testicles of the killer-hero as a symbol of courage and regeneration, the sexual jokes at the expense of the female characters through the novel (there is even the cliché of the widow with an unbridled sexual appetite), the male jokes about homosexuality, and so forth.

However, there is also an interesting fictional meditation on the trajectory of Nicaraguan national history, which concerns us here.

With irony and parodic humour and within a melodramatic register, Ramírez recalls history through personal and popular memory rather than a faithful reconstruction of real events.[13] Most of the characters, the main events and the staging where the events take place have recognisable historical referents, but these are the motor of the storyline rather than the perspective identified and the affect created. The political thrust of the novel is evident and it must be remembered that it was written after Ramírez officially cut his political ties with the dominant fraction of *Sandinismo*, the left-wing revolutionary movement which toppled Somoza. But exactly how we read the politics determines the kind of readings we might extract. Let's start with the hypothesis that there must be echoes of Ramírez's disenchantment with the revolution's outcome in the novel, however hidden, since novels are, among other things, aesthetic responses to contradictions in real life. There are indications of this in the form of the novel itself: although it is not a tragedy strictly speaking, it exhibits tragic elements, but more as a parody in the form of a simulated tragedy: the abundant use of humour, the melodramatic style, the carnival of linguistic registers, the bathos and theatricality of the whole production lightens the tragic nature of national history and indicates an ironic estrangement from it. National history is to be laughed away as inauthentic. How is this achieved?

Margarita is replete with references to Caribbean or Mexican popular culture (La Sonora Matancera salsa band, the Mexican bolero-singing Jorge Negrete and the movie star María Felix, the Mexican popular composer Agustín Lara, references to baseball, wrestling and so own). There are abundant references to aristocratic European culture too — music, furniture, clothing, and so forth — which the author references through an imitation of *modernista* writing style and the narration of the life of the fictional Rubén Darío with references to Greek and Roman cultures. Taken as a whole, these references, whether from bourgeois or popular culture, have the structural purpose of contrasting different cultural repertories linked to different class positions. But as with the kaleidoscopic 1988 *Castigo divino*, a novel with a variety of genres, themes, styles, characters, traditions and historical periods and its penchant for excessive, complex plot elements, copious reference to aristocratic or bourgeois European culture and dense intertextuality with Latin American and European literature all seems too much at times, as if the novel were as much about novelistic 'display'. There is a palpable sense of Ramírez drawing attention to his broad cultural knowledge as much as the story itself — the novel as authorial self-fashioning. One senses Ramírez shaping an ideal, cultured reader capable of recognizing the dense intertextual references and piecing together the complex plot elements. As with *Castigo divino*, this is not a novel written for his average compatriots, it is more a performance written for sophisticated international consumption.

Margarita is constructed with several nods to classical Greek culture: it begins with a quotation from Aristophanes, there are repeated references to destiny and providential coincidences, and some chapter are even titled with Greek intertexts. These references to classical Greco-Roman culture, especially to history and myth as referential-framing devices, suggests a political-ideological stance, that of framing national history within a tragicomic drama as a way to accept or adapt to it. Further allusions to the ancient classical world abound: *Margarita* is a chronicle of a destiny foretold, that of Somoza, announced through the novel by the nearness of the planet Mars, the Roman god of war — the condemnation of Somoza is cosmic and predestined:

> — 'Mars is coming back to Earth!', he shouted. (Ramírez 1998a: 51)
> — 'Trembles on your throne, tremble in your den! Mars of the crown of blood, avenger of the heavens! Your days, satrap, are numbered! Amen.' (54–5)

The procession in honour of the late Darío is an entire Hellenic recreation skilfully combined by Ramírez with images of national pride, but at the same time emphasizing the theatricality of national life:

> Night had fallen, and at each corner the funeral procession stopped so that the orators could be heard from the top of the balconies adorned with the national flag in mourning . . .

Maidens with chiffon gowns and gilded sandals, their lips painted vermillion, opened the march in two rows, sprinkling watered roses from the wicker baskets they carried on their shoulders. The corpse, dressed in a white peplos and crowned with myrtle, was carried on the funeral litter by the directors of the León Athenaeum. (315)

The epithets of some of the protagonists recall The Iliad: The Beautiful Cupid, The Caiman, The Colossal Dragon, The Lion of Nemea, The Moustache Who Sings, The Little Girl, The Earthly Light, The Tigress of Bengal, Our Lady of the Fields. During a dialogue with Captain Prío, Erwin refers again to the theatricality and popular myth of the story:

> — And that thing of being born at the same time, the sky lit with pyrotechnics, it's opera', Erwin said.
> — Their fates are crossed, in the midst of howling and great uproar', said Norberto. (202)

On the tables of the dining room of the hotel where the welcome breakfast for Darío is to be celebrated when he returns to Nicaragua, we find 'porcelain vases painted with hunting scenes, naked Diana and her hares emerging from a shady grove' (26). The image on the vase traps Diana in eternity in a repetitive pursuit. Given the time when the novel was written, when irreconcilable divisions had already emerged among the Sandinistas and the revolutionary project had largely failed, this petrified image resonates at the political-ideological level: it echoes the way the author himself took ironic distance from a repetitive national history and the inability to harmonize the fragments of the nation as he re-creates two of its culminating events as a tropical Greek tragedy. Ramirez's disappointment with the intransigence of a certain section of the Sandinistas is well-known. He admits that Sandinismo 'stopped being the renewing force with which he rose up against the dictatorship, to become a party with all the old political manoeuvres and cunning'; 'Political falsification has returned to gradually impose a form of authoritarianism that the country has suffered in the past' (Ramírez 2000: 139). And it is this loss of faith in the project of the post-revolutionary *Sandinistas* that leads him to declare: 'In Nicaragua history continues to bite its tail, condemned forever to repetition' (Ramírez, 2001b n/p). The image in the vase, then, parallels the drama of the novel and the eternal search for national redemption. In short, although history is theatrical, references to Greek culture serve to enclose the history within a tragic framework.

This idea of the theatricality of national history, its aesthetic qualities ('I have always read Nicaraguan history as a novel that only needs touch-ups' (Ramírez 2000: 135), is also reflected in the intrusive narration that calls attention to the artifice of history writing and the affective investment of the narrator in the events. Temporal leaps are announced as the narrator addresses the reader directly: 'Let's go to the table'; 'I, if you'll excuse me, have to leave Rigoberto to find him later at Hotel America'; 'Rigoberto stopped by Rosaura's house in the San Juan neighbourhood, not foreseen by me, and only now can I give you an account'; 'Listen to this pitiful train whistle', and so forth. In addition, we have old-fashioned Hollywood cinematographic clichés that recall the parodic style of Manuel Puig in such novels as *Boquitas pintadas*:

> So I allow the face of the First Lady, pitilessly made up and aged with even less pity, gaze upon itself in the swift mirror of the waters of time as the invisible fall of a stone agitates in waves the transparent surface so that she recovers in its depths the trembling image of a ten-year old girl. (Ramírez 1998a: 17)

> Let me spin the leaves of the calendar like a whirlwind; I have at my disposal an effective aid for this purpose (which you can get to know later) so that we will not be delayed in arriving at the night of April 7, 1908, very close to Rubén's departure back to Europe. (93)

The old-fashioned filmic clichés, combined with avant-garde formal leaps of time and eighteenth- and nineteenth-century realist narrative technique of directly addressing the reader, challenge the reader to ponder the veracity of the narration and become actively involved in the structuring of the novel. In the same way as in Puig's work, Ramírez highlights the highly mediated nature of cultural messages of the 1940s and 50s and their manipulation of affect, feeding into the new cultural consumption already impacting Central America at the time of the events portrayed. In fact there is a subtle wink to the shift from a

European, and especially French, materialist consumption and cultural style among the bourgeoisie to US technological advancement with references to Harley Davidson motors cycles and modern weaponry purchased by the Somozan military state.

The tragic framework is also constructed through significant juxtapositions, especially the stark difference in imagery between the abject state of the port of Colón in Panamá and the achievements of European and American modernity, which have arrived only partially in Latin America and often in pathological form. This juxtaposition is given early in the novel in the images of luxury and refinement aboard the transatlantic ship on which the national poet is sailing, described in modernist imagery, imitative of Darío himself:

> What a difference the trip between Cherbourg and New York in the imposing ship, La Provence de la Compagnie Générale Transatlantique, the Neapolitan valet attentive to his every step, the table of the genteel captain, Monsieur Daumier, where every night he had a seat of honour, wines of Rhône and Chinon, the superb 1903 harvest, the chamber orchestra from the afternoon onwards, the plaster walls of the dining room sporting images of fruit garnishes, the imposing Flemish still life images on the panels covered with rich Florentine silk, the Bohemian crystal chandeliers reflecting in shards the ebullient splendour of discreet female traffic, strings of Bassora pearls falling between curls on marble foreheads, the magical tap of a fan on lips as an invitation to flirt. (22)

But on the next page, we have the contrasting arrival of Darío to the port of Colón in Panama, related in a more prosaic style:

> the port of Colón in Panama, the cranes of the canal against the slate sky, the camps swarming with the races, Chinese and blacks in unruly hybrid mix, mosquitoes incubating in swamps, heat of tar and smell of creosote, toilet rooms for whites and blacks separate: Yankee progress, aseptic wisdom. And finally the horrors of the *Pacific Mail* [the tramp steamer in which Darío is now travelling]. (23)

This juxtaposition mirrors the tension in the first-generation of *modernistas* like Darío, repelled by the poverty, degradation and backwardness of their home countries compared to the material comfort and refined tastes of European modernity. The eternal charm of classical Greek culture provides the *modernistas* with a cultural refuge, a vehicle for aesthetic fantasy, which, at least in their imagination, helps quarantine them from both the horrors of underdevelopment and the disintegrating forces of capitalist industrialisation.

Later in the narrative, the same juxtaposition is presented in alternative form. While writing verse on the women's fans at the farewell party, Darío tells of the European inventions on display at the Paris World Fair in 1900. The narrator then parades in the mind of his fictional poet a series of contrasting images of Latin America. The scene highlights the unreality generated by its distance from the developed world:

> Inventions of the fast age besides those others, made to mitigate the desolation in forgotten landscapes . . . He remembers his first trip to Chile in June of 1886, the port of Chimbote on the arid coast of Peru where it never rains, the houses on the shore adorned with gaudy curtains that simulated groves and thickets, a bizarre theatrical scenery. (127)

And this contrast, so perverse and striking, between the culture of abundance and refinement accessible to the bourgeoisie and the wretchedness that is the fate of the poor, sustains the revolutionary project of Sandino and later the Sandinistas of the 1970s. The juxtapositions are clearly and deliberately political.

But the fictional Darío is freighted with other discourses as well, including the demystification of national figures. When the poetry-loving conspirators are discussing an apocryphal event in which the poet is in bed with a woman, it is an occasion to mock not only the impeccable image of the national hero, already impotent due to the alcoholism that has taken possession of his body, but also the very process of writing history about the period:

> — 'Everything is correct,' says Captain Prío. 'There was a black iron bed in the room with its canopy. And the incense and the myrrh were put in the perfume burners to drive away the mosquitoes'.
>
> —'The blood-stained finger seems to me in very bad taste,' says the goldsmith Sigismund. 'Can you not remove that, my dear friend?'

— 'How do you think I'm going to alter historical facts?', Rigoberto says to him.

— 'Yes, better to remove it. And worse if it's menstrual blood, as Eulalia says in the last scene,' says Norberto.

— 'What scene? This is not a scene in the theatre,' says Rigoberto. (101)

But in all this, I emphasize, there is no outright deconstruction of Darío. Ramírez has said that his purpose was not to overturn the image of Darío, but to rescue the man of flesh and blood: 'I must say that I have always been interested in the hidden side of the characters in history. Usually, one tends to reduce the public figure to the effigy of banknotes, postage stamps or statues.' (Ramírez 1998b n/p) This criticism is reproduced when the dilapidated ship in which Darío is travelling docks in the port and the poet has to be farcically lowered in a cage to the pier:

> The women throw him handfuls of flowers that bounce off the bars before falling into the water. The wise Debayle manages to catch the cage in one of its turns, and unlocking the bolt helps him to slide over the edge of the captain's boat. The flowers now find their target and strike him, soft and light, on the chest and beard. (20)

The scene is one of idolatrous ritual in a degraded landscape, which the fictional Darío himself insults and mocks as he muses on the situation, while also eyeballing a pretty woman who begins to read one of his poems: 'It's my neice', Casimiro whispers to him. 'Married?' the poet asks. 'The incorrigible Rubén Darío! She's married, very married.' (21) Popular idolatry is thus a dance between the ordinary people and the sanctified hero: both seem to need each other. The fictional Darío is positioned between his appropriation and canonization as national myth for propagandistic purposes by both the dictatorial regime of Anastasio Somoza and the Catholic Church (acutely analysed by Eric Blandón[14]), and on the other by the *Sandinistas* as anti-imperialist icon. Needless to say, Darío is also appropriated by Ramírez himself for novelistic purposes. I am less convinced, however, by Diana Moro's claim in her 2015 *Sergio Ramírez, Rubén Darío y la literatura nicaragüense*, in which she sees Darío function in *Margarita* as an attempt by Ramírez to create national heroes.

One would think that the textual evidence points more towards the opposite — his dethroning, but not as a failed myth, but more as a man of flesh and blood, admirable, but in need of rescuing precisely from mythology. Interestingly, there is no overt deconstruction of Somoza either. If anything, Ramírez strips him of his monstrosity and reveals him to be just an opportunistic and petty criminal and presents him as a 'natural' product of the political environment of the time and its over-determination by the United States.

But crimes are to be paid for and Ramírez performs a kind of aesthetic, high cultural revenge by Darío on Somoza through the metonymic displacement of the presence of Darío onto both Quirón, the mute in whom the fictional Darío inspires a love of poetry and who will play a role in the murder of the tyrant, and the ten-year old Margarita Debayle through the poem that Darío wrote on her fan. Margarita's presence in the novel, beyond her childhood phase, is nil, but her youthful beauty is meant to symbolize hope and works as a counterweight to the trajectory of her harpy sister, married to the dictator, and further highlights the complex marriage ties between fractions of the Nicaraguan elite. The juxtaposition reveals the two sides of the same country: beauty and ugliness, hope and failure, creativity and destruction. Darío and Somoza begin to mimic their own mythical images until they are apparently unable to distinguish them from reality, and the consequences are tragic: the destruction of a poet who was still in the flower of his artistic life; and the tragedy of the Nicaraguan people under Somoza's corrupt and iron rule.

How can we reconcile the tragic elements of the novel, then, with the strong dose of humour throughout? Contrary *to Got seif de Cuin!*, in *Margarita* humour is restricted to the narrative digressions, rather than to the main events; that is, those portions of the novel that serve as a relief or respite from the main action. Their functional juxtaposition is important, since this is the stuff of everyday life, only occasionally punctuated by key events, but seemingly destined to return to the same. In *Got seif de Cuin!*, humour springs not only from minor details, but also from the most decisive moments in the course of national history, even the pomposity of the central protagonist, Don Enrique. The humour in *Margarita*, in contrast, is much cruder and more visceral: the functions of the body, fornication (the comic situation of an impotent Darío in bed and the spectre of menstrual blood), the ghastly pseudo-medical operations (the removal of Darío's brain, La Caimana's sex-change operation) and the castration of Rigoberto López's dead body and his testicles preserved in a jar. One can reconcile this mood with the tragic frame in the same way as *One Hundred Years of Solitude* does. The vision that emerges from García Márquez's novel is a tragic and pessimistic version of history: Macondo is a town destined to disappear from the earth. The humour in the novel, then, works to distance García Márquez from this tragedy, to see it as an inauthentic, laughable, a tragicomic story in comparison to the Cuban Revolution which had just shown, at the time when the Colombian was writing his book, that it was possible for Latin American nations to confront American imperialism. But *Margarita* was written after the electoral defeat of the *Sandinistas*, after the split between the *Sandinistas* themselves and after the subsequent surrender of the country to multinational corporations, the IMF and financial adjustments, as Ramírez himself has pointed out in interviews. So for the author (and for the sympathetic reader), the historical balance for Nicaragua is even more bitter, reflected in the grotesque double-entendre scene at the end of the story. After the capture of the members of the plot and the castration of Rigoberto López, the author of the attack against Somoza, Quirón enters, stage left, to steal the jar containing the testicles. Quirón provides a link to Darío and artistic inspiration and thus with the hope of a rebirth of Nicaragua: when he was a child, Darío took Quirón's head in his hands and supposedly passed 'the numen of the muses' to him (32), a fact that made him a devoted aficionado of poetry, just like Rigoberto López. Later, he is left mute after a receiving a harsh beating from North American sailors for having testified against them after their drunken rape of young girls. It is Quirón who 50 years later steals Dario's brain. After stealing the bottle with Rigoberto López's testicles, the narrator relates his flight, which also ends the novel: 'Galloping along the long streets of closed doors ... the medusa of the testicles, like that jellyfish of long ago, moving, awake, animated ... heading towards the deserted brothel, towards the source of the night and oblivion, towards nothingness' (369).

How should we read the pessimistic final sentence? What might it symbolize? Is Quirón's flight to oblivion a symbol of national failure, a symbol of Ramírez's loss of faith in the *sandinista* project? Or are we to regard Quirón, as Nicasio Urbina does, as the keeper of the revolutionary flame, of memory and hope that goes from Darío, through Sandino and Rigoberto Pérez (and Ramírez himself), the two 'amulets' signifying (intelligence and creativity (Darío's brain) and regenerative power (the testicles of Rigoberto López)? (Urbina 2004: 367). I think Ramírez is too wise for such cheap symbols and the reference to a journey to oblivion and nothingness does not allow for utopian readings. The act seems to symbolize the carrying away to oblivion of a certain kind of macho revolutionary subjectivity. In addition, Ramírez inserts in his narrative a lesbian transvestite, La Caimana (based, it would appear, on the real historical figure of a famous lesbian in Nicaragua[15]) and a homosexual, Rafa Parrales, as counterpoints to heterosexual masculinity. Both figures have links to both sides — Somoza and the conspirators. La Caimana, who collaborated with *somocismo* in the past, hides the gun López will use to shoot Somoza, metonymically linking a queer ontology to the death of the worst of heterosexual male violence — Somoza and his national guards. In addition, Darío is portrayed an alcohol-pickled impotent man, hardly the image of virile masculinity portrayed in the *sandinista* revolution. La Caimana and Rafa Parrales, with sympathies for both sides — *somocismo* and the conspirators — present a double difference — their non-norma-tive sexuality (one can only imagine for the period — 1956) and their ambiguity raise suspicion rather than acceptance, and this seems to have resonance on the political level about no third space really being tolerated between *somocismo* and the liberal conspirators (and by extension, *sandinismo* during Ramírez's time in the revolution). This idea is brought out quite well by Barbara Dröscher:

> The characters who display non-normative sexual difference are presented as untrustworthy and incapable of taking their own political positions. Taking into account the fact that the story of the assassination vindicates historical authenticity and the resis-tance against Somoza, which seems here to be the only legitimate posture, the political situation appears to only admit clear posi-tions, in regard to sexuality too. In the conflict between the dictator and the liberators, as presented by Ramírez, there can be no intermediate spaces . . . ambiguous positions are defeated. The national myth of the poet-prince Rubén Darío that has been deconstructed, and at the same time substituted by the construc-

tion of a tradition of masculine liberal intellectuals, honest, yes, but defenceless. (88)

Dröscher's reading is compelling, but I hesitate to fully endorse it: Ramírez in 1998 is a much wiser and chastened writer than in the 1970s and one could just as easily posit that it is precisely this lack of tolerance to third positions that he is highlighting. Critics will make their own judgment on this. Is the one who flees in the end, then, not the author himself? The melancholic affect is striking. In fact the novel is very open and lends itself to a multitude of interpretations, one of its major strengths.

Margarita's relativization and carnivalization of national history joins a now familiar structure of feeling of disenchantment, not dissimilar to the Boom novels and their allegorizing of national failure — the balance of two centuries of failed attempts in attempting to found egalitarian and democratic nations. Like *Got seif de Cuin!*, *Margarita* shows that a nation comes to be, not its own self-appointed vision of destiny, but simply the sum of everything that has happened to it as it struggles over competing versions of national destiny, nothing more nor less; as Ramírez says: 'Perhaps our Latin American identity is in the very fact of looking for it'.[16] We can speculate, therefore, that there are at least two types of subject and their attendant affect created in *Margarita*: the implied subject that traverses the novel itself, that exists in the semiotic ordering of the text (the textual materiality), a composite of both Ramírez's authorial intention and the non-conscious sedimentation of ideology which evades authorial control; and a more opaque subject and its affect created in the imaginary in-between space between the reading subject and the textual artefact. It depends on what kind of reader activates the text. The sophistication of the text with its complex structure, shifting historical periods, theatrical staging, polyphony and dense high and popular cultural intertextuality points to at least two ideal readers: on the one hand, a cosmopolitan consumer capable of appreciating complex intertextual references and novelistic structure with a dash of 'third-world' exoticism; and a chastened, politically progressive reader looking for an aesthetic re-enactment of a failed revolutionary project — aesthetics, as compensation for abjection in the political sphere, gives way to disenchanted, nomadic subjectivity in a movement from the national to globalization, from utopian longings to the disintegration of both the revolutionary and the national subject.

Margarita exhibits a multiplicity of themes, forces and drives along with a variety of social and psychological types. Ramírez is clearly still concerned with the insurgent popular subject as historical actor as he attempts to combine the popular with the lettered elites in a process of national 'suture'. What could not be accomplished by *Sandinismo*, will now be accomplished through fiction. What sutures the novel is positive affect, which attempts to resolve the cultural and class split-distance between the lettered city (Darío and Ramírez) and the Nicaraguan under-classes through the portrayal of a redemptive national moment — the murder of Somoza. In the wedding of oral and scribal cultures, Ramírez tries to mend the tears in the national imaginary by linking Darío, Sandino and the overthrow of the dictator Somoza in a causal and unifying chain, a Nicaraguan national wholeness torn apart by both colonial and civil-war violence, but reunited through its novelization. But this ideologizing function of the novel can only achieve this sense of underlying national unity by ignoring the historical failure of radicalized lettered intellectuals to breach the gap between their own revolutionary desires and interests and those of the subordinate classes for whom they pretend to speak and act. The semantic structuring of the whole text is thus, on one level, an exercise in aesthetic wish-fulfilment. Of course this is not the only way it can be read.

Margarita begins with a quote from Aristophanes' play, *The Birds*, in which a reward is proclaimed for he who kills the tyrant Diágoras or the cruel killer of sparrows, Philocrates. The intertextuality with *Margarita* is loaded with striking parallels: the work of Aristophanes was first presented in 414 BC on the eve of a ruinous war, the Peloponnesian War, in which Sparta and Athens faced off for control over the Greek world. It was the war famously narrated by Thucydides that eventually finished with the empire of Athens. *The Birds* tells the story of a citizen of Athens, Peisetaerus, who seeks a quiet place to live the rest of his days. To this end, he decides to create a new kingdom based on the brotherly ethics of birds. Like *Margarita*, *The Birds* also fuses tragedy and comedy and gestures towards a new and purified Athens, far from politics, militarism, false oracles and control of the gods of Olympus. In this sense it is an appropriate allegory for the Somoza dictatorship and the historical desire of the

Nicaraguan people to found a true democratic culture, a sovereign territory to counteract a history of injustice, exploitation and foreign interventionism. Unfortunately, after the birds have overthrown Zeus, Peisetaerus becomes another Zeus, another tyrant, much as the current Nicaraguan president and ex-sandinista, Daniel Ortega. Thus the intertextuality reinforces the public interventions of Ramirez: 'The mechanisms of power are always the same since five thousand years ago' (Ramírez 1998b). Paradoxically, and despite such fatalistic and sombre assertions, the Nicaraguan author reaffirms his faith in a possible better future: 'We must never fail to turn our eyes to lost Arcadias, as announcements of the utopias of the future. We can't do without utopias' (Sergio Ramírez: 2001a). And this is the situation today: how to keep the pathways to a more egalitarian future open in the context of the decline of the impact of emancipatory Leftist projects. Refuge in aesthetics is a consolation, but not a solution, but then it is not supposed to be — this is art, not a political thesis.

3

The Detritus of a Revolution in Ruins
Franz Galich's
Managua, Salsa City

'When they got to the roundabout and saw the fountain switched on, such a rare occurrence, she couldn't avoid the 'how pretty it is! Right? It's like we're in the United States.'

MANAGUA SALSA CITY (20)

FRANZ GALICH (1951–2007) was a Guatemalan-born literary writer, essayist and university professor of visual art and literature who was forced to flee his homeland in 1980 after an attempt on his life during the Guatemalan civil war (1960–1996). He lived in Managua, Nicaragua until his death in 2007. His is the author of several novels, including *Huracán corazón del cielo* (1995), *Managua Salsa City* (1999; 2000), *En este mundo matraca* (2005), and *Y te diré quién eres* (2006), and three published collections of short stories: *Ficcionario inédito* (1979), *La Princesa de Onix y otros relatos* (1989) and *El Ratero y otros relatos* (2003). A novel and a book of short stories were published posthumously: *Tikal Futura. Memorias para un futuro incierto (novelita futurista)*. (2012); and *Perrozompopo y otros cuentos latinoamericanos* (2017).

Managua, Salsa City: ¡devórame otra vez! (1999), first published in Panamá in 2000, joins a sub-genre of post-1990 novels united by a feeling of disenchantment and abjection, a legacy of two

48

decades of armed conflict, *Illusions perdues*, neoliberal re-structuring and settling of ideological scores. It appears within a narrative whose main stage has returned to the city after the revolutionary romanticism that sought the reflection of the nation in the supposed purity and organicism of the countryside, a classic ideologeme that juxtaposed the rural life to the city. But although the novelistic scene has returned to the city, this is not the promise of a new utopia, but a dystopian present — a night without end — the focus of crime and poverty, the ravages of a failed historical project, a revolution in ruins. Worthy of a movie by the likes of an Alfonso Cuarón, *Managua, Salsa City* begins *in medias res* in a canteen-lounge on a Dantesque Managua night where, as the narrator says, 'God and the Devil had a game of poker and as God lost, he withdrew to the heights and the Devil remained with the right to continue governing in Managua' (10). La Guajira, a twenty-year old prostitute, heads a band of ex-*Contra*[17] criminals and serves as bait to attract unwary rich men in nightclubs so they can be led to her house or hotels where they are assaulted by the gang. She tries to seduce a former Sandinista soldier named Pancho Rana by pretending to be an upper-class girl. Rana, the caretaker of a mansion for wealthy family on holidays in Miami, takes the family's car and cruises around feigning a wealthy bourgeois in order to attract suitable girls for his amorous adventures and get away from the harsh reality of his underclass status. He hooks up with La Guajira and they take off on a night of debauchery, unaware they are being followed by La Guajira's accomplices at a safe distance in another car. Rana contemplates robbing his employers' mansion himself and running way with La Guajira. Unknown to the gang and Pancho Rana, two other criminals have joined the pursuit of Rana and La Guajira with the intention of raping her and stealing what they can. Eventually all converge on the mansion where a bloody gun battle ensues, leaving Rana and La Guajira's gang and one of the other two criminals all dead. Only La Guajira and one of the two would-be rapists survive.

In the opening to the novel, the narrator informs us that the price paid for a failed historical project is biblical:

At six in the afternoon, God lifts the oppressive heat from Managua and allows the Devil a free hand . . . It's as if thousands and thousands of dead were resurrected and began to invade the world of the living, as revenge from the afterlife in which men, women, the old, the young and kids alike all participate. Managua begins to enjoy and suffer, God and the Devil over Managua. (9–11)

The quotation that begins this chapter represents, then, one of the many subtle winks in Galich's novel, one of the many moments in which political reality is referenced obliquely, as it were: the anamorphic refraction of an original historical referent, the celebrated national poet preserved in name in the 'Rubén Darío roundabout' (9), is an ironic, acid reference to politics similar to Ramírez's *Margarita, está linda la mar*. Galich, however, does not overplay the irony by drawing attention to it or giving it full narrative function, as in Darío's inspiration for the conspirators in Ramírez's *Margarita*, with its nostalgia for national heroes, but rather positions the reference as a mere locative cue.

Finding inspiration in cinematographic technique and the genre of hard-boiled crime novels and detective fiction, Galich's thriller is peopled by the denizens of a marginalized post-war urban subculture with their popular lexicon. Yet *Managua Salsa City* is a crime novel without the presence or intervention of police, detectives or any state forces. What one notices, except for a brief mention of a traffic cop towards the beginning of the novel, is the almost complete absence of law enforcement and they certainly play no functional role in the plot. In other respects, the novel exhibits classic characteristics of crime fiction, including a body count, the frequent use of dialogue and street slang, complex, tormented and cynical protagonists, a *femme fatale*, a love intrigue, and a cast of minor characters in the form of opponents, accomplices and other delinquents. The space-time coordinates of the action, even if in a large city, are marked by an asphyxiating compression (no way out) and darkness. The atmosphere is one of fear, insecurity, sordid behaviour and often eroticized violence. References are made to corruption and big city political machinery. Morality is in the hands of the reader, never the narrator or the characters. Mothers and fathers, the family and the State (as surrogate parent) are entirely absent. Distrust reigns supreme. Thoughts are cold and calculating. We are in a world of existential orphans where anxiety, dehumanization and indifference towards the exploitation and suffering of others is the rule. All obey the one commandment that matters —

survive at all costs. The legacy of the war is as much psycho-social as political and economic. Galich's novel takes to an extreme what we find in Ramírez's *Margarita, está linda la mar,* but which Ramírez could not completely assimilate. *Managua*'s radicality operates on all levels — language, structure, rhythm— an aesthetics of the extreme compared to the stylistic and linguistic elegance and sophistication of the political gesture of *Margarita*.

Through the fusion of the narrative voice in free indirect discourse with that of the characters, we enter the chaotic, impulsive minds and emotions of the two main protagonists, Pancho Rana and Tamara, 'La Guajira'. This is played out against the backdrop of the aftermath of the disintegration of the Sandinista socialist revolution, the counter-face to the supposed success and sumptuousness of the United States, the country that historically and perversely functioned as both the promise and refuge of Central Americans, as well as their executioner: 'It's like we're in the United States' — the irony could not be more bitter. Critics have posited that the real protagonist of the novel is the language (Ugarte) or the city of Managua (Villalobos, Mackenbach) or even La Guajira (Kokotovic). For Werner Mackenbach:

> It's an allegory of Nicaragua at the beginning of the third millennium, a Nicaragua after the great political changes, the loss of utopias and amidst a crisis of values, a post-war society, exemplary of a large part of the Central American Isthmus. The fundamental elements, the true protagonists of this novel, are the language and the Nicaraguan capital, Managua. (Mackenbach 2001: n/p)

One could even add hyper-masculinity to the list (Wieser). These are all valid possibilities. In fact they all have co-presence in the novel as orienting themes. But beyond the city and the parade of abject characters and their street jargon, there is an understated tension with an oblique presence: the right to national self-determination and a relentless ideological opponent, the United States. In fact, the novel skilfully exploits the tension between the textual surface of the plot (the persecution and violent outcome) and the historical focus-background — the Real in Lacanian terms[18] — the failure of the Sandinista project, undermined by both US intervention through the surrogate Contra rebels and through sandinista ineptness in government, which left the country exposed to the juggernaut of neoliberal capitalism without having found its niche in the new global system. Confronting the Real (the collapse of the project) is potentially destructive to the psyche. As disabused realist Galich seems well aware of this and the only people who would operate this repression at the time *Managua Salsa City* was published would be those *sandinistas* and their supporters who could not countenance the fact the project had largely disintegrated. Not so Pancho Rana and the nocturnal fauna of *Managua Salsa City*. Galich, then, is a kind of diabolical ethnologist, doing his literary work within and alongside the *lumpen* proletariat, the detritus of neoliberal capitalism and a revolution in tatters.

A *Leitmotiv* throughout the novel is the play of appearances, fiction versus reality, which has resonance on both the personal as well as political level in the novelistic construct. Both Rana and La Guajira, for example, are aware of each other's fake class credentials, exemplified in their cat and mouse dialogue in which their real thoughts are placed in brackets to counterpoint their conversation. The play of masking and coquetry of the couple is expressed in the original Spanish in the urban jargon of the lower classes of Managua:

> They turned towards the East again and passed by another market, the Iván Montenegro, where the chain of motels and bars begins. Have you ever been in there? Where? In the motels! God no! Don't tell me you haven't popped your cherry? La Guajira wondered whether you should lie and how she should do it. Well, the truth is, no. No what? You're not a virgin and you haven't been in a motel? No and no. How so? I know! You haven't been in one (by force) and you are not a virgin. (ha! ha! ha!) Don't be vulgar! What I mean is I'm not a virgin and I have never been in a motel (only he knows). (This one thinks she's gonna put one over me, but not me, others maybe). Ah ha! So what is the story? Well, when I was a teenager I was raped (the story I'm giving him). What? They raped you? . . . (she thinks I'm gonna fall for her bullshit story). (Galich 2000: 21)

In a dark comedy of errors, no one, not even the robbers themselves, gets to know the other's true motives, not even after the violent and tragic outcome at the end. Only the reader, through the narrative voice focalizing through the characters, is party to the full play of charades. The reader witnesses the vicissitudes of Rana and La Guajira as they drive through the cityscape. In a fascinating article, Daniel Quirós pictures Rana and La Guajira's cruising as a mobile map of the third-world neoliberal city with its nightclubs, brothels, gaudy architecture and renaming of national monuments under successive, ideologically opposed national governments, indicative of the fragmentation and chaos of urban space, intensified under economic restructuring and the demands of globalization: 'La Guajira and Rana's drives portray the city's urban space against the grain of neoliberal spatial homogenization, exposing its unresolved conflicts, tensions, as well as a political project intent on historical erasure' (Quirós 13). La Guajira and Rana are followed at a cautious distance by the assailants with enigmatic names (Paila'e Pato, Mandrake, Perrarenca) and to the rhythm of a strident music that fills the spiritual void. Paile'e Pato y Perrarrenca are ex-*Contra* soldiers originally trained by US military forces, while Mandrake was part of the Sandinista army and Rana part of the Sandinista special forces trained by the Vietnamese.[19] What they do not know is that two other criminals have joined the pursuit determined to murder Rana and rape La Guajira. All the characters seem to live an eternal anarchic and chaotic present with the most vile motives imaginable, people uprooted in a fragmented city. And if the lives of the protagonists make sense, it is minimal. The underworld of the novel is ruled by violence, alcohol, furtive sex and betrayal, and the options are few or almost zero: 'These days you're either a politician or a thief' (Galich 2000: 46), exclaims La Guajira.

At first the relationship between La Guajira and Rana is presented as the zero point of sexual relations between men and women, i.e. abuse, exploitation, lack of responsibility, the absence of any feelings of affection. It is a story of human decadence in the struggle for daily survival. Social fragmentation and the disintegration of common goals have meant that the war and its aftermath have turned its participants into beasts who live in an environment of corruption and vulgarity, saturated with liquor, drugs, prostitution and crime. Those who live on the margins of society in the wake of post-war ideological collapse direct their energies in new directions: 'A whole generation that learned nothing other than the war, is paralysed by the problems of post-war Nicaraguan society. At most, the skills and contacts previously acquired are useful for drug trafficking or other criminal activities.' (Mackenbach 2001: n/p) The situation is not unique to Nicaragua, however, but a general phenomenon in Latin America under neoliberal hegemony, described by Chilean intellectual and educationist, José Joaquín Brunner, thus:

> In the words of Dahrendorf, they find themselves 'on the road to Anomie' (as opposed to Utopia), expressed through various forms of social disintegration and collapse of the cultural structure . . . Contemporary urban culture is saturated with these types of reactions, ranging from gangs to murder, including no-go zones, drug trafficking, violence, woundings, theft, rape and the motive-less desire to kill, as in *American Psycho*. (Brunner 1998: 130)

Nevertheless, as the night progresses, La Guajira begins to care for Rana and sees him as a possibility to change her dangerous and abject life: 'She was attracted by the possibility that this guy will grab me as his loved one. I don't care if he doesn't cuddle and pamper me all over and only uses me to fuck when he feels like it, as long as he takes care of me' (40). Rana, now under the spell of La Guajira's sexual attraction, begins to think about the possibility of taking her with him and reveals his plan to rob his own employers. Notwithstanding the dreams of bourgeois life of both, inexorably everything ends in failure and like piranhas in a fish tank, Rana and three of the assailants die in a violent shoot-out in the mansion of the wealthy family. Thus the reification and marketing of the romantic *lite* salsa music hit from 1988 with the sexualized lyrics of male chauvinistic virility, 'Devour Me Again', is re-semanticized as the horror of a city that consumes its inhabitants, at least those who live in a tributary way off the tidbits of the national bourgeoisie that has survived the war with their wealth intact: 'Post-war Nicaraguan society has been dismembered by distrust towards the other, even in the most intimate relationships. It is a society in which each is devoured by the other' (Mackenbach 2001: n/p).

What produces anxiety and which was previously connoted negatively in the collectivist schemes of the revolutionary period — namely, the isolation of the individual — seems to take a positive value in the minds of the protagonists for whom survival at all costs reigns and primary loyalty is to oneself. Individualism is now central. The country has returned to the old system of before the revolution and the class system has been intensified. The novel, then, points to the logic of self-preservation in the face of the insecurity of a post-socialist, post-utopian world, a logic that is reflected in the frankness and surprising realism of the interior monologues of both Rana and Guajira. In a stark self-portrait of machismo, Rana muses to himself:

> That's why I'm nothing, neither one thing or the other, as it says in the song we used to hear so much in those years of partying, when we believed in what they told us, now I believe only in what I carry in my balls...I don't believe in anything because I'm skinned, but I have balls and a craving to fuck or whatever, that's all. (Galich 2000: 11)

In like manner, La Guajira describes how she learned to 'market' her life:

> They took away my virginity when I was 14 years old, but since I'm pretty with a nice arse, I never got into glue sniffing, because the boys fought over me and then they gave me good things: clothes, food, drink, grass and coke occasionally. Many old men offered to take me home as their wife, but I never went for it. Not even for the rolls of money. Just for a while, they're okay, giving them blowjobs. They pay well, but I like my independence, my own business, and not depending on any son of a bitch man who for their money want to have you as their sweetheart, maid, wife and mother. Fuck off! I said to myself one day, and I started my own business, as they say now, and we've done pretty well. (54)

But this initial image of the strong woman, the head of the band of muggers, is reversed as the story goes on by presenting her as weak and as someone who seeks and needs a man to protect her and keep her. At first glance, this is a conservative and conventional element in the novel. But paradoxically it does not end like this: who survives the carnage and the collapse of meaning? Only the woman and the least macho man — 'rat face', who lacks courage, the *sine qua non* of hyper-masculinity. Doris Wieser has carried out an insightful analysis of *Managua, Salsa City* alongside Arquímedes González's *La muerte de Acuario* (2002) and Sergio Ramírez's *El cielo llora por mí* (2008). She is interested in the nexus between gender violence and hyper-masculinity and the way women are positioned in these narratives, especially in 'a country that is sadly known for its high level of intra-family violence and violence exercised on women in general' (206). Wieser focuses on the function of La Guajira in Galich's novel, especially her sense of agency and empowerment. While La Guajira is capable of coldly and rationally setting up a 'business', however sordid, which gives her an income and independence, she nevertheless falls for Rana and sees him as a possible way out of her precarious lifestyle. For Wieser, this tends to cancel the initial freedom to exercise agency and thus 'it does not produce true empowerment, as Elizabeth Ugarte attests, 'because La Guajira does not seek a change of life for women, but . . . dedicates herself to illegal activities for fun and to satisfy her vices and desire for luxuries' (Ugarte 2001: 210–11). Wieser goes on the cite Juan Murillo who sees La Guajira's willingness to betray her accomplices as guided by a 'ritualization of masculinity . . . since Pancho Rana seems more of a man and can protect her and provide for her something that the others cannot' (Murillo in Wieser 211). There is some warrant for this interpretation in the novel, but it *is* a novel and is meant to recreate typical scenarios of the Managua underclass nightlife, so it is rather curious to expect Galich to write a Wonder Woman role, which would be improbable in the fictional construct, given La Guajira's background and the situation she finds herself in. Wieser is on surer footing when she analyses Rana in relation to Sandinista ideology and 'macho masculinity' linked to 'the myth of the Sandinista guerrilla' (Wieser 211):

> Andreas Goosses analyses the concept of Sandinista masculinity based on the *sandinista* Omar Cabezas' autobiography, *La montaña es más que una inmensa estepa verde* (1982), according to which the qualities of a guerrilla basically consist of formality, honour, a capacity to block out fear, and control oneself. It is a heroic image of the new socialist-*sandinista* man as an intrepid fighter. However, in rhetorical terms it is a paradox because this image combines the supposed 'new' with a totally traditional concept of masculinity. (211–12)

Wieser goes on to highlight how most of the men in *Managua Salsa City* see rape as commonplace and unproblematic and women as objectified and without rights and that this violent past of the ex-combatants, whether Sandinista guerrillas or Contra fighters 'not only constitutes a cultural background (the concept of a guerrilla masculinity), but also a psychological one too. It is a question of traumatized characters' (214). This is personified, for Wieser, in the fact that after having sex with La Guajira, Pancho Rana has a nightmare: 'They are characters accompanied by old fears. That is why they react in such an impulsive and violent way in situations of conflict or danger' (214). The novelistic violence of the characters is thus 'a continuation of the civil war' (214).

How should the novel be judged, then, in light of this thoroughly negative image of a Central American post-civil war city? Is there anything redemptive here? Is it just cynicism? Wieser concludes that by allowing the male characters to present their thoughts in first person narration, Galich achieves 'distance' from this hyper-masculinity rather than perpetuate it, and this is the positive moment in the novel. After a period of devastating war violence, this may be an appropriate dividend. Werner Mackenbach also finds a redeeming dimension, in the figure of La Guajira:

> a symbol of the suffering Nicaraguan nation, violated by a revolving door of men, by the Somoza dictatorship and the beasts of the North and even by the Sandinistas and the new neoliberal owners ... At the same time, it is a symbol of a society in which women are the ones who guarantee survival — despite the violent destruction of the warrior-men — and in the absence of father figures. Yes, there is also another side of Managua: passion, joy of life, and the will to survive — despite everything. (Mackenbach 2001: n/p)

For his part Daniel Quirós, views Pancho Rana's stealing of the rich family's car and driving through the city as symbolic of the main characters 'appropriating the social position and movement of the Managua elites, [which] transforms their simple 'joy ride' into a subversive gesture, albeit it in a very small way' (Quirós 13). While Quirós is quick to point out that this is hardly a blow for the revolution, 'it nevertheless presents the novel beyond the fatalistic, chaotic and even apolitical perspective it is usually associated with.' (13) *Managua Salsa City* thus raises, albeit indirectly, the question of a double failure of subaltern agency in a post-war landscape. Faced with the option of exploitative jobs that afford only bare subsistence, or no job at all, the protagonists in *Managua Salsa City* thus exercise the little liberty they have — they resort to crime, unbridled immersion in drugs, sex and alcohol and, when it is convenient or the logic of the situation calls for it, violence. This urban phenomenon is not, of course, limited to Nicaragua or Latin America. Though for the lettered intellectual reader with genteel sensibilities, or for those with spare time and literacy to read such novels, the image of this slice of urban life is horrifying, within the fictional construct these characters exercise the only agency contemplated outside of barely disguised servitude. *Managua Salsa City* raises the issue of who reads these novels or who would want to read them. One imagines that for the time when the novel was written (1999), not long after the peace accords, Galich wanted to obliquely register the unresolved issue of underclass poverty and the novel seems written more for regional consumption. This contrasts with a novel like Ramírez's 1998 *Margarita, está linda la mar*, for example, written the year before, but with a complex, modernist style and an eye no doubt on the international literary market. Galich's novel thus poses an interesting question: those who need to read such novels, especially politicians and government policy makers, most likely do not do so. There is thus an uneasy tension between admiring the artistry of Galich's novel and participating in an incestuous circle of reading which will probably change nothing, but simply mirror back to us what we already know. Nevertheless, this clearly anti-heroic novel remains an open invitation to reflect on the state of Nicaragua and Central America in general. And where are these drifting survivors of the bloody denouement of the novel heading? Unlike the ending of Ramírez's novel, they flee towards the day, and perhaps hope. What else is there? We wish them luck. They are going to need it.

PART II

Traumatic Masculinities and Fantasmatic Fathers

4

The Question of the Anthropocene in Rodrigo Rey Rosa's 'Gracia'

'The ultimate function of sacrifice is to legitimize and enact a hierarchic order (which works only if it is supported by some figure of the transcendent big Other).'

SLAVOJ ŽIŽEK[20]

RODRIGO REY ROSA (1958–) is a novelist, short story writer, translator and essayist and has created and directed three films based on his fictions. He is also the literary executor of the estate of Paul and Jane Bowles. His work has been translated into English, Italian, Dutch, German, Danish, French, Portuguese and Japanese. He is currently Guatemala's most celebrated contemporary novelist. Among his best known works are *Cárcel de árboles* (1992), *Lo que soñó Sebastián* (1994), *El cojo bueno* (1996), *Ningún lugar sagrado* (1998), *La orilla africana* (1999), *Caballeriza* (2006), *Otro zoo* (2007), *Siempre juntos y otros cuentos* (2008), *El material humano* (2009), *Los sordos* (2012) and *Fábula asiática* (2016).

Constant themes in Rey Rosa's literature are incarceration, precariousness and violence. His fiction frequently centres on child characters that are placed in situations in which they achieve a certain agency, a certain equality of action, even moral superiority. Typical examples are the children in the short story

61

collection, *Otro zoo* (Another Zoo, 2007).[21] Rey Rosa's fictional children exhibit an innate, intuitive, moral strength that triumphs over the adult world that surrounds and besets them. The questions that arise upon reading these stories are deeply philosophical and ethical.

In 'Gracia' (Grace), a short story from *Otro zoo*, chosen as the focus of this chapter, the sacrificial act of a young girl — the Gracia of the story's title — raises the question of interspecies ethics, our relationship with the non-human world and the expiatory function of sacrifice. It also implicitly questions what constitutes the 'animal', here the sacrificial lamb. The plot revolves around an agreement that a Muslim, Si Abdullah, contracts with a family in the countryside to buy a fattened lamb for ritual sacrifice during the annual *Eid al-Ahda* feast, 'The Festival of Sacrifice'. Muslims celebrate Ibrahim's (Abraham's) willingness to sacrifice his son Ishmael (Isaac in the Bible) in God's name by slaughtering lambs. The lamb Si Abdullah has contracted to buy belongs to Gracia's brother, Miguel, who pays her a small amount of money to look after it and feed it, although Gracia 'didn't do it for the money':

> 'You can look after it if you want. I'll pay you', Miguel had told her the day they brought the lamb home to the house and Gracia had fallen in love with it. 'But you have to be constant. Don't tell me one day you are no longer going to look after it, because with these things, when there's money involved, it's serious; this is a business.' (Rey Rosa 2007: 31)

One afternoon, Si Abdullah arrives at the house to check if the lamb will be ready on the appointed day. It was his habit to bring small gifts for each family member, including a rose-coloured caftan for Gracia. He engages in conversation and tells stories, but soon 'the adults began to speak about mundane and remote things like the absurdity of wars, of the inexplicable (was it really?) fratricidal hatred between Jews, Muslims and Christians' (36). Once lunch has been served, Gracia asks Si Abdullah why he wants to buy the lamb. He proceeds to explain to her that it's for the sacred Muslim festival, *Eid al-Adha*, though she is unsure of what the festival represents:

'Why', she asked, 'do they call it the festival of the lamb?'
'Because they are sacrificed *en masse*', replied Si Abdullah, without noticing the look Gracia's mother, Ana, gave him.
Gracia wanted to know the meaning of the word 'sacrifice', but her mother stood up and took her by the arm.
'You'll have to excuse us', she said. 'It's getting late for school'.
As she was dragged into the hallway, Gracia managed to hear Miguel question Si Abdullah:
'But after they sacrifice it, do they eat it?'
'It's the law', replied Si Abdullah. (36–7)

On the way to school Gracia asks her mother Ana why they have to sacrifice the lamb. Her mother tries to explain the religion of Si Abdullah, but struggles to mark the difference:

'Well', Ana said cautiously, 'we have the same God'.
'But our God does not ask us to kill a lamb?'
'Yes. Well, no. Not literally.'
'Literally?' asked Gracia.
Ana smiled.
'It's a very complicated story'. (38)

Later at school, Gracia is distracted in class by 'a rickety shelf with a series of glass jars with animals and foetuses in formaldehyde' and wonders: 'Why did God not want that fawn to be born? Why did he want that bird desiccated? Did He have nothing to do with all that?'(39) Gracia's mother had asked Father Domingo at the school to explain to Gracia the parable of the biblical sacrifice, about how God had asked Abraham to give his only son in sacrifice:

That he kill him?' asked Gracia, immediately interested.
'That's it, to sacrifice him.'
'*Why?*'
'To put his faith to the test.'
'Just for that?'
'Yes. And Abraham obeyed.'
'He killed his son?'
The Father smiled.
'Well, no, but . . . ' he said. (40)

Father Domingo goes on to explain the Biblical parable and the ram caught in the thicket and when he finishes, he asks Gracia: 'And now, do you understand?' But Gracia did not. She maintains a stubborn silence, leaving the priest to exclaim: 'Goodness gracious! . . . Later on you will understand' (40–1). But there was no way. Afterwards, returning home, Gracia's mother tries to talk to her, but she refuses to speak: 'But, my darling', she said. 'Who are you angry with?', and she laughed. 'With God?' 'I don't want them to kill the lamb', replied Gracia. 'That story about Abraham was a long time ago. And look at everything that has happened since then'. Ana tries to comfort her, but she is tense and agitated: 'I'm afraid of going to hell,' she says. 'But God would not allow a child like you to go to hell,' Ana responds. But Gracia just laughs 'with a strange resentment' (41). Although we are not told, Gracia has already determined the course events will take. She has made a decision. That night, while the family is eating dinner, Ana tries to reason with Miguel about not selling the lamb, but he won't listen. Miguel turns to Gracia: 'A deal is a deal':

> 'How do they kill them?', asked Gracia.
> 'They don't suffer', said Nander, her father.
> 'It depends', said Miguel. 'If the sacrificer is an expert, in one slash he can cut both jugulars of the windpipe'. To make his point, Miguel took a knife and feigned the fatal movement. 'But they keep kicking for a while as they bleed to death'.
> 'Both jugulars?', said Nander, adopting a light tone in order to placate Miguel: 'I thought there was only one'.
> Raising his voice, Miguel contradicted him:
> 'I read it in the Internet. There are thousands of articles on the Eid al-Ahda and the sacrifice of lambs. In some countries it's become a problem'. (43)

Gracia can't take it anymore and goes up to her room and locks herself in. Before going to sleep she kneels at the head of her bed and prays to God to take her instead of the lamb.

The morning of the day of the sacrifice, Ana is watering the plants in her nursery when she hears Si Abdullah approaching in his Mercedes-Benz. As he gets out of the car, she can't help but notice that, 'formally dressed as a Muslim with an immaculate white robe . . . he really looked like a patriarch from

Antiquity' (44). He has come to the house to pick up the lamb. Pedro the farmhand leads Nander, Ana and Si Abdullah toward the pen where the lamb is being held. Ana notices how Pedro has a skip in his step, 'as if he were initiating a dance'. Suddenly everyone notices that all the pens and cages of all the animals and birds, including that of the lamb, have been opened by someone and are now empty:

> '*In-nal din!*' Exclaimed Si Abdullah. 'What does this mean?'
> Miguel ran from side to side between the pens, looking everywhere in search of some sign, some explanation. Pedro had removed his sombrero and was scratching his recently shaven head.
> 'Where did they get out', he said, 'if the gates were closed and the locks were still there?' Ana couldn't help but smile. 'Well', she said, 'I'd say it's a miracle'.
> But Miguel wasn't listening; he was in a fit of rage walking in circles in the shed: 'It was her!', he suddenly said, and began running in the direction of the house. 'I could kill her!'. (46–7)

Si Abdullah is visibly irritated, so Pedro offers to take him to his cousin's farm where there are more lambs:

> 'It must be an uncastrated male though. The age doesn't matter. We will share it with your cousin and with your poor relations. It's the law,' Si Abdullah declares.
> 'The law?', asks Pedro.
> 'The law of Islam'.
> 'That's a good law', replied Pedro.
> At the top of the path Ana paused a moment and turned to look at Pedro.
> 'Islam is perfect', said Si Abdullah. 'This country would be perfect if everyone turned to Islam'. Pedro nodded in agreement and seeing that Ana was observing them, smiled enigmatically. Ana returned the smile. 'Maybe it was her?,' thought Pedro. (47–8)

In the meantime, Miguel has run to the house and starts banging on Gracia's door, threatening her. Nander, the father, orders him to his room and tries to get Gracia to open the door, but without success. He goes to the basement and searches for an axe to knock down the door. Gracia is convinced her prayers have been answered and crouches motionless beside her bed, barely breathing, awaiting God's punishment: 'Nander raises the axe, arching back, his eyes fixed on the point where he will strike the blow. But then Ana sees the door beginning to open; standing there, barely having overcome her fear, with her little hand raised toward the doorknob, is Gracia' (49–50). Thus ends the story. We do not finally know who exactly released the animals and birds (was it Gracia? Was it Ana?) and whether the arc of the axe is detained or not — the reader must decide. But the miracle has occurred; grace has been achieved. The ending is thus a complex weave of affect: Gracia's dread, her father's anger, her mother's anxiety and sympathy and the reader's feelings of . . . what? How do we react to a story like this and its ending? With joy, foreboding, dismay?

Throughout the story we witness Gracia struggling psychologically and emotionally with the contradictions of Scripture and moral law: on the one hand, the requirement to be faithful to God, to patriarchal and contractual law, and to religious rituals at all costs; on the other, the imperative to be compassionate. Cleaved between filial obedience and compassion, Gracia feels compelled to act against the patriarchal order represented by Si Abdullah, her brother Miguel, and her father Nander, even as it signifies her destruction. There are three contracts in question in the story: the contract of Gracia's family with Si Abdullah (the sale of the lamb); Si Abdullah's contract with his God through the sacrifice of the lamb; and the complex contract that Gracia herself makes with her own ethics and with her God when she asks him to sacrifice her in place of the lamb. Gracia imposes a value system on the sacrificial ritual that surpasses the laws of the adults and the two religions — to preserve life. In this way the story establishes a tension between Law and Ethics. Only the contract generated by Gracia (not knowing whether God will approve of her actions) produces the sanctifying grace and restores the act of sacrifice to its purity. According to the established order, Gracia has committed a venial sin, but not a mortal sin. But can one commit a sin, venial or otherwise, and still achieve a state of grace? In the fictional construct, this depends on the ethical disposition of the reader. In Catholicism grace is linked to the overcoming of sin by repentance or contrition in order to arrive at redemption. But here, at first glance, this process does not obtain. Gracia goes against the will of her family, against contractual agreement, and against what she believes is God's will (the killing of the lamb), thus her preparedness to be sacrificed, literally killed. Rey Rosa's story thus raises philosophico-religious and ethical questions about unshakable faith, religious authority and the notion of sacrifice: should traditional cultural customs take precedence over life? Is there a universal injunction that protects all life, and what would ground the decision? Or is it such that you can sacrifice any life within the logic of a religious law or cultural tradition because a transcendent Other grounds the sovereign decision?

Making a religious sacrifice normally means raising something profane to the status of the sacred. But in 'Gracia' the sacrificial act through the offering of the lamb is cancelled and overcome by the duplication of the sacrificial economy represented by the actions of the young girl. The lamb is raised above the human in an ecological and compassionate inversion: the gift, that is to say, grace, is given to something considered a mere vehicle for the economy of grace of human beings in their relationship with God. Gracia is willing to die at the hands of God in order to save a lamb destined for religious sacrifice — she metonymically and literally sacrifice's herself in place of the animal; she renders the animal sacred.

The slaughter of animals is an important theme that appears in all three monotheistic, Abrahamic religions of the book: Christianity, Judaism and Islam. All have the idea of sacrifice as a pillar of their beliefs. The Bible, for example, says in Hebrews 9.22: 'The law requires that nearly everything be cleansed with blood; without the shedding of blood there is no forgiveness' (King James Bible online). In the Old Testament, Abraham has absolute faith that he has heard the voice of God and is called to kill his son, Isaac (in the Muslim Koran it is Ishmael and not Isaac), an act to which both Abraham and Isaac/Ishmael must submit. As the story goes, an angel descends from heaven and tells Abraham to substitute a ram for his son. Either way, there is sacrifice — without sacrifice, supposedly there is no redemption. The holy Muslim ritual, *Eid al-Adha*, still repeats what Christianity had sublimated in the passage from the Old Testament to the New with the self-sacrifice of Jesus Christ. To understand what is at stake in 'Gracia', let us take a short detour through the theme of the sacrifice of Isaac in the Old Testament.

How should we interpret the parable of Abraham and Isaac? On one view, it is perhaps one of the most harmful parables of Judaism and Islam: a lesson in dogmatic faith, the potential for a father to sacrifice an innocent being, his son, for a religious intuition. In Christian mythology in the New Testament, Jesus Christ sacrifices himself for us (as the ram is sacrificed instead of Isaac in the Old Testament), relieving us of the need to go on sacrificing. But the decision on sacrifice was merely suspended: the sacrificial biblical scene is repeated everywhere and in all times and places us all in the role of Abraham— we cannot shift the decision or the responsibility to some transcendent Other that grounds our ethics, not without losing control of the ethical decision itself through filiality to the sacred Law — an imagined God, a sacred writing, a state edict, a political ideology. What happens in the scene of the biblical sacrifice is an ethical breakdown: Abraham retains his relationship of faith with God, but at the price of destroying the ethical commitment between father and son. The artistic portrayal of the binding of Isaac was common in European Christian art, especially in the first half of the seventeenth century. There are many famous painterly interpretations of the scene of Abraham when he disposes to sacrifice his son. In the typically pious interpretations (Rembrandt, Rubens, Titian, Tintoretto, Giordano) the messenger angel intervenes in time to save Isaac — Abraham has given proof of his absolute faith. In Rembrandt's version (1635),[22] for example, Isaac is lying face up with his body in a passive sacrificial position, there is a look of relief on Abraham's face when the angel appears and we see the knife already falling from his hand, relieving him of the need to complete the sacrificial act. But as Hugo Reinert attests:

> As long as the willingness of the victim can be construed, the integrity of the rite is preserved. Here the efficacy hinges on an appearance of consent, on devices that conceal the exercise of force. In a liminal space between murder and surrender, sacrifice draws power from both; the blood is necessary, but so is the *masquerade*. The violence circumscribes itself, presents as something else while still drawing power from its destructive efficacy. An active kernel, wrapped in a public secret. (Reinert 2015: 256)

In Caravaggio's earlier, heretical artistic rendition (1603),[23] however, the decision to kill, to sacrifice, remains in tension: we do not know if Abraham kills Isaac or not. There is no epiphany, no happy ending. In fact, there is no outcome at all: the scene is suspended at the peak of emotional and psychological drama. Though no struggle is mentioned in the Genesis account, in Caravaggio's painting an overwrought Isaac resists; he does not willingly and submissively accept his death and the intervention of the messenger angel (who appears more human than angel) seems to leave Abraham confused. Instead of a scene of absolute faith, the messenger appears to be arguing with Abraham, who seems unconvinced, with his brow furrowed, as if the presence of the angel were a nuisance. The knife is still firmly clenched in his right hand and the other firmly on the nape of Isaac's neck. The threat of impending sacrifice endures. For Karen Wacome:

> What Caravaggio shows us is God's horrendous command fleshed out. This is what sacrifice looks like stripped of religious sentiment. Rembrandt presents us with a picture of religious obedience glorified: Caravaggio forces us to consider what we might see if we were witnesses at an actual sacrificial scene. (Wacome 2003, para. 19)

In the background of Caravaggio's painting we see glimpses of a city, a symbol of civilization, but the sacrificial scene is one of barbarism. What is communicated to us in Caravaggio's image is something about human actions rather than God's mercy. Caravaggio rejects the pious iconography and dramatizes the psychological component. Whether intentional or not, Caravaggio allows us to re-locate and re-frame the biblical scene within secular ethics, as the painting gestures as much to the future as to the past. Isaac appeals to the spectator. He is looking at us, rather than at those on whose decision his life depends — his father and the angel. It is as if he were asking: 'Are you going to intervene? Will you demonstrate your compassion?' We cannot remain passive witnesses — we are compelled to respond. The scene requires an ethical reaction; the painting requires the viewer to complete the plot. Although we cannot intervene in this particular scene, frozen in religious and artistic history, we can intervene in other scenes in real life. How will we respond? We have to take sides for or against —neutrality does not work here, it fails to signify. We have to justify our position, which involves engaging with the ethical dilemma, so too in the story of Gracia.

Although there is extensive literature that meditates on the role of Old Testament religious sacrifice,[24] in most cases it does not question the status of non-human animals in such practices. We can begin to address this lack by starting with Moshe Halbertal's understanding of sacrifice in the Hebrew word *korban*:

> In its primary use, a sacrifice is a gift, an offering given from humans to God. It involves an object, usually an animal, which is transferred from the human to the divine realm. In its second use, which emerged later, the term refers to giving up a vital interest for a higher cause. Someone may sacrifice his property, comfort, limb, or even life for his children, country, or in order to fulfill an obligation. (Halbertal 2012: 1)

In 'Gracia' we have a conflict between these two types of giving sacrifice: sacrificing 'to' (the lamb to god) and sacrificing 'for' (Gracia's self-sacrifice for the lamb). According to Halbertal, in Leviticus: 'Atonement is achieved through the symbolic substitute of the self . . . When Aaron holds the goat, and combines that with the speech act of confession, he transfers the burden of sin to the animal, which then carries it away' ((Halbertal 2012: 31). But Halbertal's account fails to make the connection between the sacrifices and offerings described in Leviticus and the implicit hierarchization of the value of human life over all other. In *The Question Concerning Technology*, Martin Heidegger refers to the categorisation of the non-human as *Bestand* —'standing reserve' (Heidegger 1977: xx). In the centre of Heidegger's critique of technological society is the idea that the non-human world is available for humans to impose their will on it, a stockpile of raw materials to order and instrumentalize (Heidegger, 'Technique and the Turn'). This has led, among other things, to the man-made ecological crisis that appears to threaten the very survival of both non-human species and our own. Impending ecological disaster, as with the scene of violent sacrifice, requires an ethical response and that response runs through the human-animal dualism. This radical separation of humans from non-humans is based on the untenable claim to man's superiority over non-human species by positing the rational human mind and certain religious scriptures as evidence of a natural separation of humans from other animals. In *The Animal That Therefore I Am*, Jacques Derrida studies certain passages in Genesis to expose religious myth's claim that it was the will of the gods that humans be given authority over the world: 'Let us make man in our image, after our likeness: and let them [note the sudden move to the plural] *have authority* [my italics] over the fish of the sea and the birds of the heavens, over the cattle, over all the wild beasts and reptiles that crawl upon the earth!' (Genesis 1:26, quoted in Derrida 2009: KL 424–26— italics and brackets are Derrida's). Commenting on Derrida's essay in *Less than Nothing*, Slavoj Žižek states:

> Derrida's starting point is that every clear and general differen-tiation between humans and 'the animal' that we know from the history of philosophy (from Aristotle to Heidegger, Lacan, and Levinas) should be deconstructed: what really legitimizes us to say that only humans speak, while animals merely emit signs; that only humans respond, while animals merely react; that only humans experience things "as such," while animals are just captivated by their life world; that only humans can feign to feign, while animals just directly feign; that only humans are mortal, experience death, while animals just die. (Žižek 2012a: KL 2940–4)

According to Catholic philosopher Jean-Luc Marion, the gift of sacrifice, *le donné*, cannot be based on the destruction of another. The sacrifice fails, is deceptive, if the values distort or do not match the primordial impulse of the Christian sacrificial act — to produce the sacred without causing harm to others, in fact to cancel the literality of human sacrifice (Marion 2011). The suicide bombers we see in the Middle East today, or the supposedly altruistic heroic sacrifice of soldiers in the name of the glorious nation or any given ideological project, do not produce sacred acts. They may be considered sacred acts within the logic of the actors who carry them out, but they lead to the death of others, which is not the meaning of the Christian parable — Jesus Christ fulfils this act for humanity; his sacrifice was destined for the salvation of others, not their annihilation. The destruction of others is the destruction of oneself because it destroys what we have in common — life and the potential for an ethical disposition towards that self-same life. The hierarchy of values needs an adjustment: life has to rise above any doctrine that requires the sacrificial death of others. Every sacrifice that destroys the good and the innocent has no right to the word 'sacrifice' in a sacred

Christian sense. That is why terrorism and war devalue the notion of sacrifice: instead of opening a path from the profane to the sacred, they close it— you cannot consecrate by annihilating others. While Marion seems accurate in identifying the pure gift, *pace* Derrida, his theory still relies on the existence of a transcendent Other and reduces Christ's symbolic function to that of a simple mediator of God's will. But for Žižek what is lost is the more convincing idea that in the biblical parable Christ gives his life — self-sacrifices — as 'a pure unconditional gift to humanity' and thus God the Father 'disappears in the background':

> if we take this gift in all its radicality, does it not compel us to read its meaning as the full acceptance of the fact that God is dead, that there is no big Other? The Holy Spirit is not the big Other of the symbolic community, but a collective which *ne s'autorise que de lui-même* [authorises itself], in the radical absence of any support from the big Other. (Žižek 2012a: KL 675–78)

It follows, therefore, that 'the ultimate function of sacrifice is to legitimize and enact a hierarchic order (which works only if it is supported by some figure of the transcendent big Other)' (KL734–5). Žižek refers to Jean-Pierre Dupuy's *La marque du sacré* (2010), in which Dupuy frames Christian sacrifice 'with a crucially different cognitive spin':

> the story is not told by the collective which stages the sacrifice, but by the victim, from the standpoint of the victim whose full innocence is thereby asserted . . . Once the innocence of the sacrificial victim is known, the efficiency of the entire sacrificial mechanism of scapegoating is undermined. (KL 791–95)

Žižek concludes that the radical break that Christianity originates lies in the fact that it is the first religion to demystify the Sacred. For Žižek, as for Dupuy, Christianity is therefore 'not a morality but an epistemology: it says the truth about the sacred, and thereby deprives it of its creative power, for better or for worse. Humans alone decide this' (KL 975). This deconstruction of the normative Christian conception of sacrifice as a foundational myth, which can only be sustained through the appeal to an unverifiable Transcendent Big Other, opens up a void: a world free of foundational myths would lack the legitimating screen for the containment of violence that religion provides through myths sustained and perpetuated by symbolic sacrificial acts, including violent ones. Nevertheless, it is a challenge we must accept from an ecological point of view. Rey Rosa does precisely this in an act of fictional insurrection, a rich and ironic inversion of sacrificial dogma.

Marion says that sacrifice, as a gift, 'is contingent upon its acceptance by the other' (Marion 2011: KL 1261–3). But if Gracia's sacrifice is not recognized as such (it is seen as a mischievous act of a well-intentioned but naive girl), if the sacrifice is not received as a gift in the fictional construct, if it is not accepted with understanding, then the only possibility is that the act is completed and sanctified by the reader. The true import of Gracia's gift, her self-sacrifice, cannot be recognised or received by other characters in the story because Gracia's family do not share her ethical concern: Si Abdullah, Nander y Miguel are all authoritarian masculine figures who conform to religious or economic contracts; even Gracia's mother, Ana, and Pedro the farm hand, are sympathetic only because they see Gracia suffering emotionally and psychologically — not because they are necessarily against a lamb being slaughtered for a religious sacrifice. Although they are understanding, they give no indication that their concerns go beyond the immediate resolution of the situation; in other words, their posture is not based on a rejection of the sacrificial economy— they simply make a temporal exception to ease the suffering of a young girl. The ambivalent position is that of God, whose hand is not revealed in the story. He is either indifferent or untroubled by her sacrificial gesture, since he is not given narrative presence by Rey Rosa beyond invocation through Gracia— he does not intervene (lest one make a claim that Gracia is a vehicle for God's will, which requires not only a leap into faith, but also a claim with no textual evidence). By transposing a scene of sacrifice into fiction, Rey Rosa removes the sacrificial economy from the will of God. In the biblical narrative — call it fiction or not — the will of God is omnipresent, even when he does not act. However, in a literary fiction (despite the Christic imagery of sacrifice), God is absent and judgement, as Gracia expects it, is not passed — it remains suspended, in the hands of the reader. As with the viewer of Caravaggio's *Abraham and Isaac*, we choose to kill or not kill.[25]

We are in the era of the Anthropocene, now an epoch of *longue durée*, in which man has quasi-biblical power to change global climate. The killing other species, even if just for purely ritual purposes, is part of a broader environmental assault, an assault for which we are responsible. If we did not realize this before the Industrial Revolution, it is no longer the case — we are aware of our species impact. Our projections onto the non-human world are anthropomorphic fantasies in which we have sought a faithful reflection of ourselves, our self-mythologizing through comforting patterns we claim to decipher in the non-human. The question of the Anthropocene, then, is also the question of immortality, our desire to continue living in some way beyond our expiration date. It is this mixture of religion and desire for immortality and entry into some heaven in a state of grace which drives us, but it comes at a price.

Meanwhile, we witness through a fictional construct, a pure ethical moment, the profound beauty of Gracia, a subjectivity in full ascension. Gracia's act of sacrifice makes no sense in an economy of exchange — either monetary or symbolic — which, according to Jean Luc Marion, requires a 'counter-gift': some compensation, whether recognition or salvation. But Gracia's gesture is to the void: although one is tempted to say she is making a gift of herself to God, in Rey Rosa's story her sacrificial gesture is in reality directed to the lamb, itself unconscious to human motive — it is not a volitional agent in the human ritual. The refusal of Gracia to participate in the rite by withholding the sacrificial object (freeing the lamb), interrupts both the economy of financial exchange and the sacred sacrificial economy. Her pure ethical moment is beyond simple material abnegation, beyond the abnegation of happiness, beyond even the hope of recognition of her act — Gracia invites her self-destruction and seeks no salvation. She sees herself as neither martyr nor victim — there is no textual evidence to support either claim. The real scandal of the story, therefore, is not the broken commercial contract, but rather a young girl's ethical agency exposing the tenuous charade of patriarchal hierarchy on which the act of sacrifice is based and legitimated. The true sacrifice is revealed, left naked: ethical obligations are sacrificed to the Law. We will have occasion to return to the question of the non-human animal as a moral subject with rights towards the end of Chapter 7 on Claudia Hernández's short stories.

5

The Boy in the Bubble
Eduardo Halfon's
Manaña nunca lo hablamos

'Corazón, no moleste.'
MAÑANA NUNCA LO HABLAMOS

EDUARDO HALFON (1971–) is a Guatemalan writer who has lived in the United States since he was 10 years old when his family went into exile. He subsequently returned for eight years to teach literature before returning to the United States. His grandfather was a Holocaust survivor. His life not only speaks of cosmopolitanism, but also multiple marginalities: from his country of birth through exile, from the dominant Catholic religion of Guatemala due to his Arab-Jewish background,[26] from the majority of the poor Guatemalans due to his middle-class upbringing, from his partial distance from US society as an immigrant, and of course, from his own childhood and his formative years, whose emotional architecture he attempts to recover in fictional form. He has published numerous collections of short stories, including *Siete minutos de desasosiego* (2007), *El boxeador polaco* (2008), *Clases de hebreo* (2008), *Clases de dibujo* (2009), *Los espacios irónicos* (2010), *Mañana nunca lo hablamos* (2011) and *Elocuencias de un tartamudo* (2012) and (2017). He has also published several novels: *Esto no es una pipa, Saturno* (2003), *De cabo roto* (2003), *El ángel literario* (2004), *La pirueta* (2010), *Monasterio* (2012), and *Signor Hoffman* (2015).

This chapter analyses the collection of short stories gathered under the title *Mañana nunca lo hablamos* (Tomorrow We Never Discussed It), which are linked by an adult narrator remembering his younger self during key affective moments of his idyllic childhood, his paradise lost. *Mañana* is thus a quasi-novel in fragments. It begins with 'El baile de la marea' (The Sway of the Tide) and a man recalling his childhood when his father took him to the beach:

> The black sand was boiling. I had to walk quickly over stones and shells and pieces of plastic and large mangrove seeds until my feet felt the cool balm of the tide. There was no one in sight, save an old Indigenous man up to his waist in the waves, fishing with a scarcely visible line that he cast out and then wound back in between his palm and his elbow.
> 'Give me your hand,' my father said. 'The tide is very strong'.
> 'I don't need it'.
> 'I said give me your hand'.
> We stood there a while, in silence, him holding my hand rather brusquely, both up to our knees in the fresh foaming water.
> 'I drowned in this sea.' (Halfon 2011: 15)

The father explains to his son that he was his age when he went swimming a bit further down the coast and got caught in a rip and drowned. He was rescued and revived by a US marine who had been sunbaking on the beach. The narrator remembers his feelings at that moment: 'I felt something in my stomach that today, now, I would describe as fear' (17). He also remembers having wanted to ask his father 'what would have happened if the soldier hadn't been there . . . who would have been my father . . . who would I be without my father?' (17). They leave the beach and the narrator recalls: 'For a while afterwards I could still feel the sway of the tide against my legs' (17). This tide can be read metaphorically as much as affectively, something we will return to at the end in the final story, 'Mañana nunca lo hablamos'.

The opening story sets the tone and style for the rest of the book. We are taken on a literary journey through the memory and affects of a young child as narrated by his elder self, an emotional evocation of a child's upbringing in a Guatemala convulsed by civil war as the army fought left-wing guerrillas until the boy's family's eventually goes into self-imposed exile in the United

States. The adult narrator sympathetically attempts to re-capture his confused feelings at the time of key events prior to the family's flight: a visit to the beach with his father, the great earthquake of 1976, a skirmish between the army and a guerrilla cell in his school, the killing of a frog through displaced anxiety, the deep sense of loss occasioned by leaving Guatemala, the pain and sense of abandonment when it is discovered he has a tumour on the brain, and a chance sighting of a female guerrilla involved in the kidnapping of his mother. Halfon's fictional construct has much in common with his own autobiography, which he freely acknowledges.[27] The ten partially disconnected stories are linked to each other through a common first-person narrator, common characters, and a consistent urban ambience, as well as the emotional reactions of the child to the idea of death and the constant threat of violence outside his cocooned existence. The play of focalization between the older and younger narrative selves and the sparing use of free indirect discourse wonderfully evoke the unresolved emotional tension and attachment that the narrator has to his past.

What stands out in the opening story and from then on is a heightened sensory reading experience as the child's vivid emotional recollections create an intense fictional affect, which is passed on to the reader through a cleverly mounted focalization through the child's feelings before they are retroactively assigned a named emotion by the adult narrator. This effect is achieved, in part, through the use of colour and sound. It is also created through its tension with narrative temporality — not the succession of events, but the switching between adult and child to intensify feeling. But perhaps there is also a more delicious tension: the narrator's family is middle-class, entrepreneurial and opposed to the left-wing agenda of the guerrillas seeking to radically change the country. This class positioning of the young child against the backdrop of war creates a secondary emotional tension between the political stance of the adult narrator and his own family. The tension is not expressed in didactic discourse, however, but alluded to in descriptions of the modest wealth that helps quarantine the family both economically and racially from the mass of poor Guatemalans.[28] One strongly senses the moral position of the narrator because of the way conversations are framed and description is focused through the racialized consciousness of the privileged middle-class boy. Yet, and as in

Rey Rosa's story and Claudia Hernández's fiction, discussed in Chapter 7, the narrator does not pass moral judgment: moral and ethical judgements are thrown to the reader to make, which then creates a further possible tension between the class position and political leanings of the individual reader, instinctively moved to take a position one way or the other on the background politics to the plots themselves.

In 'Polvo' (Dust), the young boy discovers a world in one day when he bonds with his Uncle Benny, a volunteer fire fighter, who takes him along to help victims of the 1976 earthquake: 'that other time, a more innocent and perfumed era, much whiter, when it wasn't rare to see a child walking alone through the streets of the centre — a chaotic, disarticulated centre in ruins — with his two little hands on his head so that an enormous and slippery fire helmet didn't fall off' (30). The disturbing 'El poder de la euforia' (The Power of Euphoria) finds the boy returning from school with his report card still sealed, terrified that it is bad and he will incur the displeasure of his parents. But he discovers that his grades have improved remarkably and his mother is very pleased, after which he runs to the garden and proceeds to kick around a large toad before putting in into a plastic bag and smashing it against a brick wall: the toad pays the price for the boy's displaced anxiety. In 'Quieto a la orilla del lago' (Still Beside the Edge of the Lake), the boy spends time after school with Rol, an orphaned young man who since he was a teenager has lived at the back of the family garage and works as a general handyman and occasional child minder. Rol had been raised by his grandparents ever since his mother had died giving birth to him. One day he has a furious argument with his grandfather who points up to the sky and says: 'your mother would be weeping black tears over you' (66). Rol leaves, eventually finding a home of sorts with the boy's family. Through Rol, and as in other stories, we get a glimpse of the other Guatemala, the Guatemala of the poverty-stricken peasantry, of Indigenous Guatemala. Rol talks of his childhood: 'My grandma made tortillas and my uncle grew corn and beans. They were really poor, but I never noticed, or perhaps it didn't really matter that much' (66–7). Rol relates how he used to go fishing early in the morning and sell his catch around the local villages: 'Imagine, young fella, my happiness. What else could I ask for?' (67). The boy sits watching Rol work a sewing machine to repair a shirt: 'I felt again the same tingle in my stomach that I felt each time I imagined Rol's infancy on the lake and a string of fish over his shoulder, the fishing line wrapped around a pole; it was that same tingle I used to like to feel or perhaps I didn't like to feel, but which I didn't fully understand' (67). Through free association, the narrator is linking the sensation back to the time when he was on the beach and saw a fisherman in the waves and his father told him about drowning and being revived. The sensation is linked to the indescribable feeling that the idea of death evokes. The story ends with Rol recounting how the same day of the argument with his grandfather he was fishing by the lake when there was an earthquake: 'It shook so hard that I fell to my knees in the mud. Imagine. And even though I was scared, I just stayed there stuck at the edge of the lake as the day rapidly became night and the sky began to cry down black sand all over me' (69). Rol imagines his mother's disappointment.

'Muerte de un cácher' (Death of a Catcher)' portrays the boy at seven years old. He seems to have a tumour on his brain and cannot stand the constant pain that embitters his life and interrupts his studies. He struggles to absorb the difficult truth of an event that has been constituted by the very incomprehension of its occurrence — the death of a baseball catcher whom he idolizes. The internal struggle and the feelings of alienation, accentuated by the pain, are staged by means of changing perspective — one moment through the narrator as an adult, another through his childhood self. The change of perspective, moving in and out, creates the tension by means of which the narrator takes pity on himself as a child. The story begins with a masterful visual image:

> Professor Ochoa had remained in mid-sentence, a subject without a predicate, the piece of white chalk floating in the air and a hand adjusting the mysterious black pirate patch that had us all entranced, even more entranced than his cryptic way — a very large eight and a capital letter — of signing our written works after grading them.
> 'Now he's crying, teacher,' someone repeated.
> 'What?'
> 'Now he's crying. Look at him.'
> I felt the weight of thirty gazes.
> 'Are you crying, boy?'

> I didn't answer. I couldn't speak because of the pain. All day I
> had a stabbing pain in the back of my head. (45)

The reader never learns for sure whether the child has a tumour
or not. That tension is not resolved in the story, nor in a way does
it really matter. Through shifting focalization, the decisive events
that established the architecture of the narrator's affect as a child
are revealed. His memories are imprinted on his body: 'a sharp,
deep pain.' He also remembers how due to the tremendous pain,
he ends up peeing himself at school and washing his pants with
lots of water to hide the stain: 'Water hides everything, lad,' says
the teacher. Without a clear definition of the cause of his ailment,
the child is taken to a clinic where he is subjected to a series of
tests, but without definitive conclusions. A dispute arises
between the clinic's medical experts, who think he has a tumour,
and the boy's paediatrician, who thinks he doesn't. Faced with
the paediatrician's denial, the child is taken to the house where
he is placed in his bed in the family room to watch the broadcast
of a New York baseball game, which is just about to begin:

> On the television appeared the green and argillaceous image of
> the still empty diamond of the Yankees. Few images I liked as
> much as that one, so promising, so clean, so pure, so resplendent
> with greens and browns and whites. While the Yankees players
> ran from the dugout towards their positions on the field, the
> Guatemalan commentator, Abdón Rodríguez, was saying some-
> thing I couldn't hear, but which obliged my dad to sit up a bit
> straighter on the sofa. The silence seemed strange. At the begin-
> ning of each game when the players were running out to their
> positions, Abdón Rodríguez always played the same music
> ('Velvet Hands', by Bebu Silvetti, I would find out years later).
> But he said nothing. (57)

Baseball provides the child with the image of an ideal world, an
escape, an obsession that distracts him from his illness, a substitute fantasy object of heroicity and accomplishment onto which
to displace his illness. But that day, the famous Yankee catcher,
Thurmon Munson, a real person from the 1970s, dies in a noto-
rious plane crash. They give the news on television before the
baseball game. The child (like 'Gracia') struggles to understand
what is happening, although he realizes that the routine of the

famous Guatemalan baseball commentator and the tone of his voice have changed and his father has fallen silent. The great homerun hitter Reggie Jackson is crying. When the father tells the child what has happened, he is overcome by grief, which manifests as numbness, as if his last hope were extinguished. He turns his back on the television and stares out the window at a sombre image of nature:

> My brother approached me a little and asked me what had happened, but I said nothing. I felt the ice pack behind me, somewhat warm, sunken and squishy on the pillow. I took off my glove. I took off the black catcher's mask. I no longer understood, or did not understand everything, or I preferred not to understand, but I did understand that I did not want to see a great homerun hitter crying anymore, nor did I want to see that empty plate any longer, now without a catcher, and then I turned my gaze towards the window. The sky seemed a caramel colour. Outside, with each gust of wind, a long cypress branch scratched across the glass. A soft steady drizzle was still falling, as if reluctantly. (58–9)

Thus the story ends. The child dies a symbolic death, unable to translate his dejection into meaning. There are three witnesses to the event: the adult narrator, the reader, and nature. 'Water hides everything, lad,' the professor had told him that day at school. Now an abysmal drizzle falls, 'as if reluctantly,' and rather than hiding everything, as on the day he peed his pants when in extreme pain, the water now mirrors his despair. This is a complex, visual linguistic staging of affect, a small narrative gem. Did the boy have a tumour? What happened afterwards? We don't know nor does it really matter, as the whole point of the story is the recreation of a 'structure of feeling.'[29] The lack of plot resolution further heightens the affective tension. The story ends as it began, *in medias res*. The lack of a conventional denouement, an ending without closure, mirrors the emotional scarring still evident in the adult narrator. We only know that he survived because he tells the story. His childhood self was doubly injured with both the physical illness and the death of his idol, both foreshadowing his own possible death. In the story, the images, the atmosphere created and the linguistic materiality are perfectly harmonized: 'To paint not the thing, but the effect that it produces,' urges Mallarmé.[30] The image of the final paragraph is therefore a kind of neo-existentialist portrait of despair and nothingness in the style of Albert Camus: in the face of the child's *Illusions perdues*, nature demonstrates its mute and intransigent presence, silent witness to the disaster — the child's harrowing understanding of his situation falls on his emotions with all the heaviness of the world: 'I no longer understood, or did not understand everything, or I preferred not to understand, but I did understand.' As readers, we are witness to a kind of breakdown and transformation of a subjectivity, the interruption of its integrity, incapable of framing its solitude in a conceptual explanation, which adds to the melancholic feeling of solitude and abandonment. The family security is no longer the unbreachable bulwark against the world, which had provided a tenuous bond with hope. The boy gives up the solace of baseball and turns his eyes to the window; he turns his back on his hopes. His pain is directed towards external objects — the glove and the baseball mask, the symmetrical harmony of the baseball field and its colourful diamond — 'so promising, so clean, so pure, so resplendent' —, all symbolic substitutes to fill the existential void and obscure the feeling of a childhood paradise loss. The final scene is the collapse of meaning, which the child only senses indirectly: 'A soft steady drizzle was still falling, as if reluctantly.' A radical event without logical explanation (as we shall see in Hernández's short stories), a serious illness, the loss of a symbol of hope, all highlight our inevitable mortality and the spectre of death that peers through tears in the symbolic fabric of our lives. The scene of writing, then, is Halfon's attempt to stage the way fragmented memory, especially of traumatic moments, can haunt the present, especially through moments of affective intensity linked to unresolved contradictions on both the psychological and emotional level.

In 'La señora del gabán rojo' (The Lady in the Red Coat), we attend a habitual Sunday family outing at a well-to-do steak restaurant also frequented by the father's friends and acquaintances: the atmosphere is festive with marimba bands, good food and conviviality, but nevertheless 'we always sat so that dad would have the best view of the main door ("I like to see who enters")' (74). We are in the time of kidnappings of the middle-class and business people for ransom. The narrator subtly alerts us again to class divisions with the physical description of the marimba players, 'dark-skinned, expressionless' (75). Suddenly, the atmosphere changes:

> 'That woman over there in the red overcoat,' whispered my father, but I wasn't sure if to me or my mother or to the whole table. Then, with a gesture with his chin toward the door, he whispered again: 'she was one of the guerrillas that kidnapped my father.' (75–6)

The narrator re-tells the story of the grandfather's kidnapping, his confinement and his eventual release after a hefty ransom is paid. The narrator remembers what he felt the moment he looked towards the woman: 'I always imagined kidnappers as a child imagines villains: smelly, fat, hairy, with only two or three teeth, with greasy faces covered in warts and pimples and scars. Never as I imagined a lady, even less a lady who was beautiful, dressed to the nines, resplendent in her red coat' (76).

In 'Corazón, no moleste' (Heart, Be Still/Sweetheart, Don't be a Bother), the boy recalls the Scandinavian Anderson who worked as an engineer in his family's textile factory. He had arrived to install new machinery, but after being offered a contract decided to stay and started a family with an Indigenous woman with whom he had two kids, one who looked like him and one like her, who was partially disabled and with deformed hands. Anderson mysteriously disappears after eight years leaving behind his wife and children, but we are not told why, though the narrator muses on the sudden disappearance of people during the civil war.[31] Soldiers are seen around the house protecting the family. Anderson's wife arrives with her two daughters. She is there to request money from the narrator's father. She seems to have been crying, but we are still not told what has happened to Anderson. The boy amuses himself by inking dates onto a piece of paper with a stamp. Suddenly, the woman's disabled daughter, the one who looks Indigenous and whose hands are mere stumps without fingers, approaches the table to play with the boy: 'Sweetheart, don't be a bother', (111) her mother says. The boy is repulsed by her appearance and tries to avoid her:

> She was wearing a pale green dress which was too short, short white socks that were wrinkled, brown orthopaedic shoes. Her

bent, little legs were the same colour as mud. Her gaze seemed dark. She never stopped smiling at me with her mouth half open and the tip of her tongue sticking out. There we were for a while, looking at each other in silence until all of a sudden, as if someone had tripped her, she fell on the carpet and instinctively, without thinking much about it, I stepped back and bumped over one of the leather couches. 'Behave yourself, my son' [...] But what is behaving yourself in that situation and at that age faced with two frightful stumps? Why didn't her mother come over and pick her up and take her away, far away from me? Why didn't anyone help me? (111)

The memory is narrated by the adult, but the focalization is once again through the child's feelings. The class distance already established throughout the stories in *Mañana* is reinforced once more by the young boy's sense of revulsion at something outside his perfect world. But we soon find that this is merely a novelistic ploy as the adult narrator subsequently redeems the disabled girl. She kneels beside the table and with her mouth drags a piece of paper in front of her. With her teeth she extracts a black charcoal pencil from the mug and begins to draw on the paper. The boy is curious to know what she is doing, but feels a certain disgust. Eventually, Anderson's wife gathers up her children, receives a cheque from the boy's father and leaves. The father asks the boy if he wants to say goodbye, but he is too absorbed in the paper the girl was drawing on and goes over to the table to take a look: 'It was perfectly square. The girl had filled it with dozens of vertical and horizontal black lines, all faint, but very straight, as if drawn with a ruler' (113). This is the point where the adult narrator most distances himself from his childhood self, highlighting his cloistered existence and haughty privilege. The childhood idyll is graphically counterposed to the arrogant classism upon which his world is built.

This distance from the majority of ordinary Guatemalans reaches its culmination in the final and eponymous story, 'Mañana nunca lo hablamos' (Tomorrow We Never Discussed It). The story is initially set in a private school as the children are leaving on buses in the afternoon. We learn there has been a fire fight between the army and the guerrillas and a clandestine guerrilla headquarters in a house up the hill from the school has been blasted to rubble with several guerrillas killed. The police escort the buses out of the zone. Without direct ideological commentary on the violence, the focus is once more through the young boy's gaze and feelings as he stares uncomprehendingly at the scene of confusion in 'the afternoon light the colour of *mate* tea' (117). The narrator moves back in time to relate how 'the first shots were fired at ten in the morning' and how in a farcical scene, his teacher, 'Miss Jenkins, a plump, affable North American, gave a big smile and got us to sing songs in English, while she accompanied us by clapping her hands while the machine guns sounded' (118). As the bus pulls away, Oscar, the boy's friend, is 'pointing at a dirty shape, surrounded by people, in the scrub and the mud on the side of the ravine — a woman's dead body' (119). The skirmish between the army and the guerrillas is the final straw for the parents and they decide to sell up and leave for the United States. As the boy and his brother prepare for bed, their father enters the room and begins to rail against the situation in the country:

> He spoke in a disorderly and babbling way of the fighting that afternoon, of the workers in his textile factory, of mum's nerves, of the North Americans, of the Indians, the guerrillas, the communists, of the kidnapping of my grandfather fifteen years ago, of the bars they had to have installed on the windows, of his new bodyguard. (120)

The father informs the boys of the decision to leave the country. The parents are unwilling to say for how long, in spite of the boy pressing them, but there is an air of finality: 'The house', my father said, getting to his feet, 'is already sold' (122). The next day school is cancelled and the boy amuses himself in the morning watching English-language children's videos sent by one of his father's golfing friend in the United States. The videos provide a welcome distraction and allow the child to drift back into his fantasy of harmony: 'I felt a kind of serenity in the liturgy of returning to see those same cartoons and hear those same tunes' (123). Along with the English language, a small apartment the parents maintain in Florida and other references, we see the penetration of US culture into the region and the United States as the preferred escape route for middle-class families under threat. In the afternoon, the boy calls his friend Oscar and is invited over to his house. They get together in the tree house and read newspaper articles describing the combat of the day before. They stare at the photos. One catches the boy's eye. It shows a dead guerrilla, a guitar and a TV screen in the house with a photo stuck to it. The photo:

> is like a passport or ID card photo of a dark-skinned man with Indigenous features: 'According to the authorities, this guerrilla was identified as Roberto Batz Chocoj, a bricklayer from Patzún, Chimaltenango.' At the bottom of the page there is a photo of a group of military personnel. (125)

The boy sits staring at the faces of the soldiers, 'so dark and so Indian, like the face of the guerrilla with the guitar and the television. I didn't understand. The soldiers are also Indigenous? Wasn't every guerrilla an Indian? Who was a guerrilla, then?' (125). Back at home it is evening and the boy is pensive. His grandparents and father are drinking whisky. His grandmother decides to take the boy for an ice cream. Out of the internal domestic space, the boy is once more exposed to the vicissitudes of encounter. While he is mooning over the different pastel-coloured ice creams sold in the store at the park, the narrator sets the scene:

> the little grey donkey eating grass, his carriage off to one side, empty . . . a barefoot and shirtless kid, more or less my age, was sweeping the floor with a grass broom. Finally my grandmother entered and a young, squat, somewhat dark-skinned Indian woman, dressed in white and pink uniform, politely asked me what I would like. (129)

The boy watches as a cone of his favourite mandarin-flavoured ice cream is prepared and handed to him. Suddenly the spell of the idyll is interrupted:

> When she passed it to me over the fridge, I noticed her dark little chubby fingers stuck in my ice cream. I felt sad. I thought of not accepting it, of not eating it, of asking to be served another, a new one, a clean one. But it was mandarin ice cream and so I made an effort to forget the image of the daubed fingers. My grandmother paid the bill and tossed a few coins to the boy with the grass broom and we left. (129)

The narration throughout all the stories creates a pastiche of Central American, middle-class creature comfort propped up by the labouring poor — ice cream vendors, street sweepers, shoe shines, fishermen, dirt farmers, restaurant staff, soldiers, guerrillas, and so forth, providing the underlying tension of racialized class warfare and US ideological penetration, not dissimilar to that identified in Galich's *Managua Salsa City*. Halfon ironizes the role assigned to the underclasses — the Indigenous soldiers and the ice cream incident — the political sub-text gnawing away at the affective idealisation of childhood, the story the author wants to tell without telling it, referencing it obliquely, which the best of post-war fiction does. Halfon wants Guatemalan history to be legible, but not in an overtly didactic way. The child's idyll is further destroyed as his maternal grandmother begins to grill him on who his favourite parent is. The child can't decide:

> 'Every child has his favourite', she assured me brusquely, 'the dad or the mum'.
> I bit the edge of the cone.
> 'And I believe that your favourite is your mum, you know.'
> Suddenly the mandarin didn't taste of mandarin. It tasted strange . . .
> I never worked out what it was. The mandarin-flavoured ice cream, the smeared fingers of the young, uniformed woman, my grandmother's naïve questions, or the sudden accelerations and hard braking in that beautiful old Mercedes, or perhaps all those little drops of whiskey that I took out of my grandfather's glass. But as soon as we had stopped in front of my house I pushed open the heavy door of the Mercedes, kneeled down on the gravel and threw up. (131)

The child's nausea is now resonating through the whole book. Everything is now contingent. He has one final piano lesson with his teacher before the family's move to the United States. They say their goodbyes. That night the child has a nightmare in which the dead guerrilla in the news photo with the television and the guitar enters the house and kidnaps his mother. He wakes up agitated and his father comes in to sooth him. When the boy calms down, he lays out his preoccupation:

What's a guerrilla? . . .
Ah ha!
Well, the guerrillas are responsible for all this trouble.
What trouble?
All this trouble, he firmly whispered, the trouble in front of your
school, in the factory, in the streets, in the whole damn country.
Are the guerrillas Indians? . . .
Yes, he said, his gaze towards the window.
But are the soldiers Indian too? (137–8)

The nonplussed father pauses and then begins to explain that it is too late for discussing these matters, gently pats him on the knee and says it's better to talk about it tomorrow. As with the priest in Rey Rosa's 'Gracia', paternal figures struggle to impose their explanatory narratives on the young because of the glaring logical contradictions in their arguments.

Throughout the stories hands play a prominent symbolic role, always as comfort, parental security and communication and never raised in anger in the boy's world. The father tucks the boy in, leaves and turns off the hallway light: 'Everything turned black, immobile. Soon the morning arrived and tomorrow we never discussed it' (138). The unavoidable contradictions in Guatemalan society are thus best left unsaid in this privileged world; so too paternal hegemony. One is struck by the irony of a middle-class family with a background of racial-religious persecution (the Jewish grandfather), perpetuating the structural racism against Indigenous Guatemalans, the same Indigenous Guatemalans who populate the army that protects those self-same middle classes, the same Indigenous Guatemalans who lived that other genocide.

Mañana nunca lo hablamos had begun with a father and son alone together on a deserted beach, holding hands, and ends in similar fashion, with the father trying to calm the son's confusion in the face of a massive social contradiction, soothing him with his hands.[32] The tide in the very first story now resonates on the political level in the final story as it signals the turning of the tide with the recrudescence of the civil war and the presence of urban guerrilla cells. The scene of fear and mortality at the beginning of the book returns with a vengeance on the eve of the family going into exile. Halfon, like his Guatemalan compatriot Rey Rosa in *El material humano* and *Caballeriza*, writes from the life experiences of the Guatemalan middle-class, even if their politics have moved them to the Left in adulthood. It is both atypical and refreshing to have dissident authorial point of view constructed from within this class fraction because it allows for a more complex portrayal of the tensions which drove the uprisings, tensions which have not gone away. As with most of the fiction analysed in this book, there is an ending, but no closure.

6

Carlos Cortés'
Larga noche hacia mi madre
The Labyrinth of the Past

'Like writing, fatherhood is a form of suicide in the service of
immortality, and every son an executioner.'

SILKE-MARIE WEINECK

CARLOS CORTÉS (1962–) is an award-winning Costa Rica novelist, poet, journalist and essayist. Among his major works are the
novels *Encendiendo un cigarrillo con la punta de otro* (1986), *Cruz de
olvido* (1999), *Tanda de cuatro con Laura* (2002), and *Larga noche
hacia mi madre* (Long Night Towards my Mother, 2012), the
novel studied in this chapter, and the recent novella, *Mojiganga*
(2017). He has also written three collections of short stories,
Mujeres divinas (1994), *Crucificciones* (2004) and *La última aventura
de Batman* (2010), and several collections of poetry as well as a
book-length essay, *La gran novela perdida. Historia personal de la
narrative costarrisibile* (2007). In 2016 he was awarded the prestigious French Government medal, Knight of Arts and Letters.
This chapter reads *Larga noche hacia mi madre* for both its decon-
structive drive against motherhood and masculinity and the
way narrative voice is constructed in an exercise in authorial
affect.

A writer in his 30s returns to Costa Rica from France to be at the
side of his mother as she approaches death. It is an occasion to
recall the family history. Returning home is thus returning to the

past and its painful truths, especially the troubled relationship that the tormented narrator-son has had with his mother:

> My mother wanted nothing more in life than to be a good woman, a good mother. I hated her and I don't know if I still hate her. I hated hating her and I hated knowing that I hated her. In some place between her madness and mine it served me well, it fortified me, and it saved me from something worse, although it would condemn me for the rest of my life. I hated her as my umbilical cord to the worst in me myself, to my father, the horror of his death and the secret that shrouded him like a mortuary veil. (Cortés 2012: 13)

The protagonist's mother is forced to walk the son's narrative tightrope between her portrayal as monstrous, but also as a sympathetic figure redeemed as the novel closes. The relationship is described by the narrator as one of mutual-loathing and disgust as the mother's health and mental stability begin to fail her until she is interned in a psychiatric hospital. The story thus has as its diegetic centre the conflict between a mother and son. All narrative lines converge in this tension, including those pertaining to the father, since the novel also deals with attempt by the narrator to establish the truth about his father and about the mysterious circumstances of his premature death just before the narrator was born.

As with Phé-Funchal's novel, *Ana sonríe* (discussed in Chapter 9), a family's troubled history is reconstructed through memory. The mother's death in an asylum is received by the son as liberation from his inner struggle with her, a struggle he remembers beginning the first day she turned up at his primary school in the middle of the day, dishevelled and incoherent, asking about his welfare. Her deteriorating physical condition and her internment for mental illness folded like a cloak of guilt over the family: 'That is what she turned into and that is what we turned into too' (13). The son muses about whether he secretly wanted her death: 'I never forgave her for not being the perfect mother that I had dreamed for myself, although she was not responsible for not being able to be that; I began to ferment that deep resentment in school, when for the first time I was ashamed to be her son' (13). He also recalls a sense of growing loss as he realises that 'the other half of my life, which remained alive after my father's disappearance, started to abandon me' (14). The narrator adopts a cynical and sarcastic tone towards his own recollections, comparing his life to a 'soap opera or a survival manual for orphans' (16) and labelling his reaction to his mother's illness as 'a little stupid and pathetic, and it is. But I lived it that way. I hated my mother because it was the only act of freedom I could enjoy in those days' (18). As he passes through adulthood and is able to come to terms, at least partially, with the catastrophe that has been his relationship with his mother, he comes to a realization:

> I have discovered that she was right and I continue to be inside her. I look at myself in the mirror, I repeat her gestures and I make the same mistakes as her with regard to my father, myself and others. (19)

> Mum and I both shared what I detested in her. We were both born after our fathers had died, we had brittle finger nails, crooked teeth, which were an embarrassment when smiling, and we felt stupid. Or they made us feel stupid. (24)

The narrator-son goes to hyperbolic extreme in linking the intensity of his hatred for his mother to that of the children of a woman who committed suicide in Srebrenica. He sees a cipher of his mother's fate in the newspaper article on the unfortunate woman who hung herself because she could not save her husband from the Serbian slaughter of Muslims and was subsequently despised by her own children: 'It is the fate of humanity in a woman's body, like a rabbit or a piece of meat hanging from a butcher's hook . . . on her hand you can see her wedding ring and it is not an irrelevant fact, but at the time I did not pay attention' (27). The woman had left her children at the refugee camp where they waited for her until the next day, but she had disappeared: 'They searched for days, weeks, until they recognized her in the photograph of the woman hanged. They could do nothing but hate her. When it is empty, hatred fills the heart. I know' (27).

As the novel progresses, we also learn of the family falling on hard times, a middle-class family reduced to poverty and frequent charity and the early death of male members of family, a kind of family curse. The task seems to be not only to remember the family past, but to try to survive it, the dissolution of its ties and the loss of its economic security. Yet the novel is not just about the narrator's bitter family memories, it's also about memory itself: its lacunae, its self-deceptions, its silences and its nature as a process and an archive shot through with affect. Though Cortés has been quite forthcoming about the autobiographical elements of the novel,[33] it is self-referential rather than autobiographical since it is a stylised literary evocation of a past told through a highly emotional register. Rather than concern ourselves with the parallelisms with Cortés's real life, then, we can look at novelistic technique and what the plot can tell us about the play between memory, mourning and forgetting around family trauma and the way our parents shape us, for better or worse.

At the end of the first chapter, 'La mujer de las gavetas' (The Woman of the Drawers), the narrative voice directly addresses a 'you', whom we presume to be the reader, and explains why he returned to be present during his mother's last moments since he supposedly hated his mother so much: 'You ask me why I came, who made me do it, what feeling could be more than an atavistic indolence to play the role of the good son. I tell you that I wanted to know if I loved her, if I still held for her a feeling similar to love' (33). The narrator has thus laid out his case for hatred and it is up to his interlocutor — the reader — to pass judgment on his tale. Though the major disappointment of his life seems to be his hatred for his mother, and the fact that she couldn't be the perfect mother he desired, the novel is nevertheless driven forward as much by the narrator's attempt to know and understand his biological father, Quique, who had died before he was born. In fact the novel turns on a key event: the mysterious circumstances of Quique's death. As the narrator excavates the past, an image of the father slowly emerges through small discoveries of letters, albums, photos, postcards, court records and newspaper clippings found hidden in drawers, through isolated phrases, imaginative connections and through the narrator's aunt as her mind also starts to falter and the secrets you swore to keep come tumbling out:

> She only did it many years after the real events, once they seemed far off and she supposed that they couldn't hurt me. Once she was dead, I came across her hidden and unimpeachable papers and there they were — the raw facts. Upon reading them I understood what my mother had wanted to say to me,

telling me things without telling me — ' . . . my pure love, my good love . . . ' — my father's fairy story. (38)

The retelling of the parents' stories thus becomes a deconstruction of both motherhood and masculinity, as well as the tragic outcomes that are possible in dysfunctional families. A sense of melancholy, solitude and loss are marvellously sustained throughout as the novel explores the anger, the pain and the release to be found in revisiting the past in order to try and let it go.

From what the reader can piece together, the father, Quique, was shot to death before the narrator was born, when the mother, Lily, was five months pregnant. Thirty-five years later, after having returned home to see his dying mother in the psychiatric hospital, the narrator randomly flips back through associated memories. He recalls how his mother had had a long, promising nine-year engagement followed by a disappointingly short one-year marriage. He recalls being brought up by his grandparents, how his grandfather Fernando was the person he loved the most in the world and how most of the other males in the family tree were failures at business and marriage, most dying at a relatively young age. He also relates how the family fell into genteel poverty, and how he and his mother, a former teacher of adult education, were forced to live off her disability pension and the charity of their extended family (a double-edged sword) after her health deteriorated. When aunt Nena dies she leaves a strongbox with important papers which uncover the story of how Quique had had a long-time affair with Tongolele, a nightclub woman, who had tormented his mother during her years of engagement to Quique. The narrator links this to one of the possible reasons why his mother lost her sanity. On another occasion, his mother had claimed that she had been raped during a bus trip to Venezuela when she went there to study adult education after the death of her husband. But the son doubts her story. The parents' marriage was dogged by sexual dissatisfaction, which the mother had subsequently revealed to him: 'Your dad and I did not enjoy sex. I didn't know how to please him in bed and he was dissatisfied with me. Our intimate life was very frustrating for me' (31–2). The narrator wonders whether this subsequently coloured the way she presented the past, and whether:

the convulsive, obsessive delirium she suffered when she was depressed produced guilt at having had an occasional boyfriend whom she had sex with in Venezuela, six years after being widowed. The puritanical, demure widow that she had promised to be, especially for me, transformed that episode into a threatening shadow imbued with unnameable sexual connotations. (32)

In spite of what the narrator would have us believe about the cause his mother's illness, and what he himself had believed earlier in his life, towards the end of the novel he relates his conversations with Aunt Nena, who reveals the family secrets: 'mum's depression was not the result of mourning for my father, as I had thought in my romantic version of the facts, but due to the post-traumatic depression caused by the hysterectomy that she suffered in 1972. The gynaecologist forgot to prescribe the hormonal treatment with birth control pills' (180). And if this more prosaic reason were not enough, the narrator reminds us that his mother and aunt Nena had also lost their brothers when they were only in their 50s. As the narrator builds the case for his hatred towards his mother, then, he simultaneously undermines his own complaints by listing the obstacles his mother faced throughout her adult life, including paying for his private education, 'with many sacrifices' (50), on a public employee's salary. He declares that his hatred 'is not against her but with her or against others, against the shadow [of his father]. We orphans are like this. There is hatred within us' (69).

The novel is set up by Cortés to establish a difference between the emotions felt by the narrator at certain points in time in the past and their retrospective framing and narrativization in the present. The effect causes a fictional splitting in the narrative consciousness, a technique observed in Escudo's *El desencanto*, Halfon's *Mañana nunca lo hablamos* and in Phé-Funchal's *Ana sonríe*. The novelistic interplay between the narrator's earlier self and his narrating self creates the tensions and contradictions of unresolved emotions of loss, regret, hatred and self-loathing, the bitterness that drives the narrative. This is further accentuated by the semi-autobiographical nature of the novel itself — the novelist's relationship with the two fictional versions of himself. Cortés mounts a clever literary portrayal of personal anguish by staging a conflict between judge and accused — between the narrator and his mother. But ultimately the main conflict staged is between two sides of the narrator's own being, registered in both his conscious thoughts and his feelings, as if he were seeking self-justification for his attitude: 'To say that I hated her is a bit melodramatic. What did I feel for her? The impossibility of us ever forgiving each other. During my youth I hated three people, the last of which was her. My longest loving hate' (17). The narrator becomes the accused as much as his mother, with whom he has much in common, including the fact that both were orphaned from their fathers while their mothers were still pregnant. But the similarities run much deeper:

> Over the years, with absolute terror, I discovered that she was right and that I am still inside her. I see myself in the mirror, I repeat her gestures, I make the same mistakes as she, with respect to my father, myself and others; the same bad relationship with the body, the perfect predisposition towards failure, vulnerability with others or the lack of responsiveness. (19–20)

In Lacanian terms, the non-coincidence of the narrator with his mother is in actual fact his non-coincidence with himself. The narrator-son identifies with his symptom, since he cannot do away with the memory and the influence of his mother in his life, the only solution seems to be to identify with his mother. At the centre of the story, then, is an antagonism within the narrator himself — not only his tortured relationship with his mother, but also his father, or rather the figure of the paternal, and his relationship with himself expressed through guilt and longing for the lost years. In her ground-breaking study on fatherhood, *The Tragedy of Fatherhood: King Laius and the Politics of Paternity in the West* (2014), Silke-Maria Weineck situates the problem of fatherhood from the viewpoint of the son and how the father in Western culture and literature is revealed as both all powerful but also vulnerable, fatherhood as essentially always a tragedy in the making, a house of cards. What is this father figure?: 'Freud's answer is nothing less than stunning: it is the *Gschnas*, a comical hodgepodge, an imitation object of great repute that on closer inspection consists of worthless trifles. As the image of power, fatherhood is not just a simulacrum, but a hysterical (!) joke' (Weineck 2014: 169). One of the foundations of patriarchy is paternity — the ability to produce offspring. Commenting on the plays of Heinrich von Kleist, which delve into paternal uncertainty and the problem of the law and the institution of the family, Weineck declares:

> Kleist's work demonstrates that, ultimately, the ideology of fatherhood needs no fathers, and that it can so reliably reproduce them precisely because it does not need them to take any specific form. They can be installed through the language of blood or the language of the law, visible or invisible, disembodied or spectacularly physical, heroic or decrepit, human or divine, filicidal or sacrificial; they will resist and survive natural catastrophes as well as all social, legal, or ideological reforms as long as we are governed by those desires we imagine fathers can grant— the desire for protection that is inscribed into us during childhood; the desire for reconciliation that is part of our historical heritage of history itself; and, most importantly, the desire for conflict that renders oedipal even the most radical critique of the patriarchy, and hence in the very moment of its success can only reproduce the most powerful father of them all, the dead one. (162)

As in Hernandez's stories, then, the dead don't stay dead for long in Cortés's novel — they live on as zombies haunting the living. If the book's semi-autobiographical memoir departs from a primal event — the murder of the father — this is a father in name only, a fantasmatic figure, 'that blank space' (Cortés 2012: 16). The image of the father slowly emerges through narrative flash-backs and piecemeal revelations, references to old photos, newspaper clippings (he was a star football player) and the recollections of family members, aunts and uncles and a grandmother, who figure strongly in his upbringing. The truth is finally revealed when Aunt Nena dies:

> My father, in fact, as I suspected, was scattered in several graves. Not his physical body, but those that composed a contradictory memory that was gradually being revealed to us, as if his body had been conformed in successive changes of skin throughout its scarce and infinite thirty-five years. The men of his generation had lived more at my age; several lives, and he had several. My mother was only in one of them; I was in none. (25–6)

Similar to the theme of masculine violence and family dysfunction in other writers in this book, the narrator rounds on the male figures in no uncertain terms: 'Useless, good for nothing, incapable, vagabonds, thick, idiotic, were the cries I often heard from their mothers, sisters and cousins, upon remembering them, not always with endearment' (52). But the narrator is himself now both son and father, with two daughters and a divorce behind him. He has to embody the symbolic father as well as the real father, that fatal split. The difficulties in assuming the position of the father are highlighted in Chapter 4, '(Daddy's Sunday)', in which the narrator reflects on his own paternal function. He has been living in Europe and is separated from the mother of his children. After six months back in the country, the affective distance between him and his daughters has remained the same: 'We share a mutual distrust' (66). The distance is due, in part, to the bad relations he still has with his ex-wife, but also to three and a half years overseas. He gets them to agree to a lunch outing and thinks about how to behave with them, but he feels like he is just going through the motions:

> I don't know how to be a good father. I have no idea, though I think I've always tried. After the time that has elapsed I am no longer a family presence and my daughters resent it. There are already eight and ten. In a few years they will be adolescents and it will be too late. (66)

He senses himself repeating, unwillingly, the same cycle of the absent father figure and the guilt and remorse the role entails. As he drives through the city with his daughters, they pass by the old neighbourhood of Freses where they first lived in an apartment when the girls were much younger. The ten-year old recalls living in the apartment and her younger sister replies, 'Me too' (67). The recent past is recalled through objects, sights and smells, an affective cloud that momentarily unites the father and daughters, but then quickly falls away. In free indirect discourse, the author further entangles the narrator in his own labyrinth of memory and regret, reinforced by his youngest daughter, Adriana, inventing her own past memories of the apartment, which irritates the narrator-father:

It's not true. Adriana doesn't remember or can't remember. She was four years old when I left the house and sometimes she tells me that she only remembers me wearing yellow pyjamas. Or were they blue? She was two years old when we left Freses to the new house in Sabanilla. I could say to her: how can you not remember when I took care of you every morning, from eight to noon, and prepared lunch? How can you not remember? She doesn't remember. How are you going to remember, if you were a baby? (67)

This play of recollections goes on a bit further until they arrive at the housing estate where the girls live with their mother. The narrator recalls the precise number — '67' — as if to test his memory: 'We part with a stolen kiss. I don't want to say goodbye, but they've had enough for a Sunday' (68).

The narrator cannot fulfil the conventional societal script for fatherhood; few fathers can. But women are also indicted for being complicit in the perpetuation of male gender roles and privilege. Aunt Leonor is described by the narrator as: 'of course, the perfect mother, the perfect wife, the perfect daughter, the perfect housewife, and the perfect future grandmother. Any mother worthy of the name should be like that. Her words made me want to vomit' (57). This slavish submission to gender conditioning and devotion to men who don't deserve it is something we shall see portrayed in Phé-Funchal's novel. It is also highlighted in the figure of Aunt Lillian and her relationship with a married man, Don Álvaro, and the kind of domestic shrine she prepares for him in her house:

At one corner of the house she organised a kind of bar in which she arranged bottles of whiskey, glasses, a bowl of ice and chips or any other type of snack. We were never allowed to enter there, much less eat any of the sandwiches, breads or sweets that Aunt Lillian prepared for Mister, as Danny called him with loathing. (60)

Aunt Lillian and Don Álvaro were never married due to the excuses that 'Mister' gave for years, one that the narrator declares 'men have given for centuries so as not to have to get a divorce or in order to hide their cowardice behind masculinity' (61).

In *Larga noche hacia mi madre*, it is also space — house, rooms and corridors as boundary markers, asylum, landmarks in San

José — that serves as one of the organising principals that allows the narrator to catalogue his bitter memories. During his child-hood he lived for a while on his grandparents' farm and then in several rented houses until a two-storey house of wood was constructed in San José. The house takes on the aspects of a personality with its objects, its spaces, its secrets, a house worthy of a Faulkner or a García Márquez, but unlike these writers it is not raised to allegory in order to stand for a historical epoch. Though the vagaries of Central American economics are refer-enced through the uncle's misfortunes working in Panama and the eventual loss of the family home due to debts, the house is mostly the theatre of domestic dysfunction. It holds the secrets of the paternity of an orphaned child (the narrator-son), the villainess seducer (the absent father), the loss of family prestige and material wellbeing and the slide down the class ladder symbolised in the humiliating treatment at the hands of chari-table yet mean-spirited relatives. The house they lived in became dominated by one of the narrator's aunts, Flora ('charged with looking after me', 18), and her insufferable sister, Lia: 'Flora and Lia saw us as a burden, mother and I, even if they lived in a house built by mum and Aunt Nena, and we put up with them and hated them as one puts up with and hates family' (54). These inci-dents all elicit emotion and affect from the reader in a melodrama worthy of nineteenth century realism. The desperate fear of *déclassement* has genuine reference in so-called developing coun-tries like Costa Rica, in which poverty has an altogether different meaning and effect than in Western European-style social democ-racies. Family support networks are supremely important, but they come at a cost: in the case of the narrator and his mother, constant humiliation at the hands of haughty relatives. Aunts and uncles play the role of villains or heroes according to their own mis/fortunes and their own treatment at the hand of affective others.

Larga noche is also a sociological and cultural history of San José and its environs. Its direct cultural, geographical and histor-ical references are only properly decodifiable by a local reader: they have cultural and historical depth — they are not mere geographical references. One, in particular, calls attention to itself: the Chapui Psychiatric Hospital in San José, scene of the novel's opening and finale. In her review of Manuel Solís's *Memoria descartada y sufrimiento invisibilizado*, a treatise on the short, 1948 civil war and its aftermath, Monserrat Sagot captures the effects of unreconstructed masculinity and political violence on Costa Rican society:

> It was not possible to speak of the consequences of that violence within the family, because the family is a sacred and safe space, paradise in a world without a soul, as Talcott Parsons said. What happens there, stays there, most of the time unnamed, even if there are aggressions of all kinds, the product of authoritarian tyrants in the home. (Sagot 2013: n/p)

Authoritarian masculinity in the domestic sphere thus mimics on an affective level the murders, political discrimination, clientelism, nepotism and electoral fraud in the public sphere, linking personal suffering and its mental pathologies to a generalised societal disenchantment and climate of fear. Referring to the significant increase in psychological conditions after the civil war, registered in Solís's book, Sagot writes: 'the alcohol, the beatings, the dangers and the brothels were intermixed with politics in that period . . . more than brave and heroic fighters for democracy, there were a lot of men with authoritarian masculinities, aspiring caudillos, quarrelsome, drunkards, with serious personal and family problems' (n/p).

Regardless of the civil war, the portrait of domestic and public violence as communicating vessels with unreconstructed masculinity at the centre, matches the reality observed elsewhere in Central America.[34]

Larga noche leaves us, then, with a feeling for the fragility of life and relationships, the enormous pressure under which some individuals labour, the damage done by a failure of communication, the ravages of heterosexual masculinity, and a story of rough redemption — the mother is redeemed by the author and the reader, if not by the narrator. But there is no possibility of ultimate suture, with the mother or otherwise. The gap between full affective reunification with the mother and antagonistic separation is the very basis of the general social symbolic order, regardless of any particular conflicts. The novel is about finally coming to terms with this untraversable divide. Nevertheless, the two final chapters end with a reconciliation of sorts. In the penultimate chapter, the son recognises his mother's difficult life circumstances: 'She endured widowhood alone, the judgment, the shame, the dispossession, the suffering and honour. She endured me and she loved me. She endured herself and never realized that it was worth it' (Cortés 2012: 192). The opening of the novel had sent us back in time through the son's memories until it eventually closes back in on the opening scene. A familiar enough technique in novelistic and filmic story-telling, here it serves the cathartic purpose of allowing the reader (and the implied semi-autobiographical author) to redeem the mother in the final chapter when the narrator-son withdraws and the mother is given the final word through a dream sequence. Her Parkinson's drives her delirium as she recalls the hardship she suffered through most of her life, including a cheating husband, the loss of the family's livelihood, the indignity of charity, and her illnesses. In a final act of reckoning and exorcism, she addresses her son through their bodies:

> I rip the straitjacket that muzzles my lips. The mute eyes, the tears and the skin sewn from secrets that scream. My cries break the thread of blood that binds my mouth. I cast out all the words through the pores of your body. Words, just words; words are all I am. Goodbye my son, my life, my love. You are alive. Everything is okay. (196)

Does the son hear the mother's soliloquy, or is it only us readers? Does it ameliorate his hatred? We don't know. The novelist seems to pardon the mother, but not the narrator. We feel an emotional response to the mother's rebellion against the circumstances that shaped her life and her wasting away. Feelings toward the son, however, are mixed. While the narrator is not unusual in magnifying the emotional impact of momentous family events when he was a child, he seems indecently late, as an adult heading into middle age, in finally giving his mother a break, especially knowing that she had a mental illness which clouded her behaviour. Along with the author, who built this fiction, be it semi-autobiographical or not, the reader releases the mother from the narrator's condemnation. But is the narrator redeemed by his own self-criticism? Not really. This makes the dance between Cortés and the fictional account of his past all the more interesting. Whether the novel amounts to a deconstruction of motherhood, is therefore debatable. But at a minimum, it strips bare the ideological accretions of maternity and highlights the duress and social pressures under which many women labour and the emotional impact it has on both them and their children. But the novel clearly deconstructs masculinity, a particular Costa Rican version marked by autobiographical experience.[35]

In the last chapter the narrator assumes his mother's voice, but even before that, he comes to realise that the father he idolized, but never knew, whose absence he displaced onto his mother and converted into hatred, was a rat. The counterweight to the failures of paternity is a story of women who hold the family together, who endure and teach the narrator how to endure, how to survive, to know that life is worth living. In a recent interview, Cortés commented on his sense of kinship with fellow national Juan Hernández, author of the recent *Dígame quién soy yo, madre* (2016, Tell Me Who I Am, Mother). He declares the novel to be an acid commentary on, among other things, 'the social construction of the family institution as a repressive system' and the 'character of the mother as a weapon of mass destruction' (Cortés 2017: n/p). But what he most wants to concentrate on in Hernández's novel are certain phrases which he considers he himself could have written in an earlier period of his life, including: 'My family is a faraway country to which I never wanted to return'; 'and you say that word that I never found out how to pronounce, dad'; 'loves kills'; 'mum's the cancer that invades me'; and 'I tried to do away with the legacy of my family many times.' Cortés goes on to link these emotions to a broader sensibility he claims to share with Hernándéz: 'My name is orphanhood . . . From the real, physical, metaphysical, symbolic or acquired orphanhood litera-ture is born, or at least this literature that Juan and I — and others — write' (ibid.). It seems obvious, then, that Cortés has not been able to move completely through the process of mourning for a paternal relationship that never happened and a maternal one initially based on hatred. Everyone, of course, has a right to their own melancholy, but it is surprising, since *Larga noche* seems precisely to perform a cathartic function vis-à-vis an extremely difficult and emotionally wrought relationship between a mother and son. In the meantime, we have an emotionally charged account of family dysfunction, which has as one of its motors the problems of heterosexual masculinity in the figure of the father, a common theme throughout this book.

103

PART III

Gendered Bodies and Affects

7

The Difficulty in Burying the Dead

Claudia Hernández's *De fronteras*

'los ahorcados no se ven mal porque cuelguen del techo, sino porque la lengua cuelga de ellos.'

'MEDIODÍA DE FRONTERAS', CLAUDIA HERNÁNDEZ

CLAUDIA HERNÁNDEZ (1975–) is a Salvadoran author of several books of short stories, including *Otras ciudades* (2001), *Mediodía de frontera* (2002), *Olvida Uno* (2005), *De fronteras* (2007), 'La canción del mar' (2007) and, *Causas Naturales* (2013). She has recently publisher her first novel, *Roza, tumba, quema* (2017). In this chapter I concentrate on the short stories in *De fronteras* (Of Borders). I proceed by briefly examining several of the stories from the collection to then concentrate on 'Carretera sin buey' (Highway Without an Ox) and the question of animal ethics. Originally published in 2002 as *Mediodía de fronteras* (Noon on the Borders), the title taken from one of its stories, this extraordinary little book was subsequently re-issued in 2007 as a collection of sixteen short stories and re-titled *De fronteras* to reach a wider public. Three stories were omitted from the original to conform the stories more to the central theme of borders and death. The 2007 edition is the version commented on in this chapter.

Like most of her short story collections, described by Linda Craft as 'surrealist explorations of a violent and dehumanizing reality' (Craft 2013: 181), Hernández creates a powerful affect of a time and a place — post-civil war El Salvador, an affect born of the consequences of violence, socio-economic precarity and criminal impunity. But though the stories in *De fronteras* are placed in and generated from the local, they transcend national borders in dealing with a universal problem — the psychological and emotional legacies of violence. The 'reality' of the fictional world created by Hernández is exceeded with a kind of gothic horror, but one in which a space is created where grief and anxiety can be explored. The stories register the result of traumatic societal violence and the inability to adjust to the disaster by being expressed on a hyperbolic, surreal level: an unidentified body found in a kitchen and advertised in the lost-and-found in a newspaper, a man without an arm who gains a rhinoceros as compensation, a family living in a sewer, the creative disposal of a dead grandfather, a buzzard as a member of a human community, a man trying to change into a dead ox, a suicide who cuts out her tongue first and feeds it to a dog so as not to horrify others with her death. The mutilated body is central in many stories. But the animalization of human beings also sits alongside the humanization of animals. The grotesque plots are infused with black humour and the uncanny and delivered without moralistic judgement in a laconic, matter-of-fact style. Echoes of Kafka and Swift proliferate.

But these surrealist explorations of dehumanization and the seeming impossibility of mourning have their own uniqueness. The only way to process that which cannot be processed psychologically or emotionally is for a transformation in subjectivity and ethical disposition, subjectivity split into two, as it were, so that one half can still function in a rational, orderly way while the other makes the journey across the boundary or threshold. Hernández works to isolate affect and ethics by removing strong spatio-temporal cues, such as names of regions, cities or recognisable historical events. The reader just knows that this is a Latin American country. *De fronteras* is also one giant ellipsis — the underlying causes of most of the deaths are hidden, so too causal or didactic explanation of the surreal reactions of the characters to violence and death, which might send reception to quickly into specific local political issues — the historical-political background of the place of production of the short stories is El Salvador after the civil war. The social and political landscape is recognisable across Central America, aptly described by Ileana Rodríguez as one of a crisis of governmentality:

> At the turn of the century, the novel of national construction yields to the novel of national destruction that is dedicated to staging an anti-heroic, 'disposable' social subject, composed of demobilized combatants and state cadres displaced into unem-ployment , the informal economic activities of all kinds or migration to other places. Plots unfold with a luxury of details about the bureaucratic entanglements that have as an effect the paradigmatic disorganization of the whole previous order. The fundamental theme of these texts is the ungovernability of people living within localities formerly organized as national states and now relegated to a status of territoriality, areas re-colonized within a regime of higher colonization . . . people respond by ignoring all regulations or state social reason and exist as a parallel force in an alternative, marginal way of life. (I. Rodríguez 2006: n/p)

Hernández seems to want us to contemplate the persistence of routine in face of horror and the daily presence of death and the issue of the inability to mourn in the traditional way — mourning as a necessary and natural reaction which must then be traversed lest a person be trapped in perpetual melancholia. In 'Mourning and Melancholia', Freud differentiates melancholy from mourning. Whereas 'mourning is regularly the reaction to the loss of a loved person, or to the loss of some abstraction' (Freud 243), melancholia is pathological because it cannot accomplish the work of mourning, cannot re-direct libidinal energy from the lost object to a new object and move on. The melancholic remains fixated on the lost object, which he or she internalizes and makes the centre of his/her identity. For Freud, melancholy also means that the lost object can no longer be consciously perceived or properly framed as such and infuses itself in all aspects of the melancholic's life.

In Hernández's short stories there seems to be no horizon beyond a generalized sense of loss, and the daily task of burying the dead is complicated as they don't want to leave (or can't leave). The stories automatically invite philosophical and ethical readings as much, if not more, than sociological and political analysis. They deal, among other things, with the boundary between sanity and madness, whole and part, stasis and change, past and present, inside and outside, human and non-human, and so forth. The stories speak as much to threshold experiences as simple border crossings and we should read them in that register: under what conditions can a threshold be crossed?

In the opening story, 'Molestias de tener un rinoceronte' (The Bother of Having a Rhinoceros), the narrator relates how after losing an arm (though no explanation is given as to why), he suddenly finds himself being followed by a devoted little rhinoceros: 'he keeps approaching me so much that people think he's mine. So does he' (C. Hernández 2007: 112):

> Missing an arm is uncomfortable when you have a rhinoceros. It gets harder if the rhinoceros is small and playful, like mine. It's annoying. The people of these beautiful and peaceful cities are not accustomed to seeing a boy with one arm less and a surplus rhinoceros jumping around him. One becomes a spectacle in boring cities like this and you have to walk through the streets and put up with people looking at you, smiling at you and even approaching to talk about how beautiful your rhinoceros is, sir, you didn't buy it here, right? (11)

The man becomes a public sideshow. Why? Perhaps because he is identified, like being tattooed, with a collective traumatic event that everyone recalls, but struggles to speak about or process and so in Freudian style, displaces it onto a less threatening topic, a substitute — a cute little rhinoceros. It is thus with biting satire that the narrator declares that the 'people of these beautiful and peaceful cities are not accustomed to seeing a boy with one arm'. It is important to note that everyone — both the man and the townsfolk – all see the rhinoceros. The delusion is universal in the town. Or is it? Since the one-armed man is also the narrator, the delusion may just be of his own psychological-emotional making. We don't know and it is to Hernández's credit that the physical existence of the rhinoceros is not questioned within the fiction. The man tries to give the rhinoceros away to other people, but they refuse to take as it is obviously the rhinoceros is deeply attached to the man. At one stage, deeply annoyed, the narrator tries 'to lose him in a region dominated by the night' (12), but to no avail. Like a crypt on the psyche from an unresolved trauma, 'nobody will take a rhinoceros from a man who lost his arm' (13). There are hints that a violent event may have occurred, which has caused collective denial through trauma.

'Un hombre desnudo en casa' (A Nude Man in the House), involves the daily appearance of a mysterious, ghost-like man with no clothes in the narrator's house without explanation and who sits staring out the window. The narrator-owner makes him coffee and leaves the sugar on the side in case he is diabetic, that way he can decide if 'the hour has arrived to begin to end his life of prohibitions and privations' (29). They converse and the narrator expresses his discomfort with the man's presence and his possible death in the house: 'If you prefer, I can die elsewhere,' the man replies. 'It makes no difference,' the narrator replies, 'on your skin and in your gaze it would be written that you began to die here'. The man re-appears everyday for a month and they repeat the same dialogue. Finally, the narrator gets up the courage to ask the man what he is always looking at or for through the window. Suddenly: 'He looked at me with terror and sadness and left through the window. I haven't seen him again' (30).The spell was broken. But what was it? What was the man trying to come to terms with? Was he looking for an appropriate place to die or how to die an acceptable death? What did the question prompt such that the man disappeared for good and the story ended? Was he waiting for permission to finally die or was he already dead, a soul in limbo? Or was he re-enacting the scene of a murderous bullet? We simply don't know.

In 'Invitación' (Invitation), the first-person female narrator is on the point of going for an outing when suddenly she sees herself as a child passing by the front of the house. Her young self calls to her to come out and play, but she doesn't want to. The narrator then sees herself as an old woman ordering her to go out with her younger self. Wrapped in just a sheet, she follows the young girl only to get lost in an unknown part of the city. When she makes it home, she finds that she is locked out of her own house, now inhabited by her younger and older self. In this tale of divided identity, the person on the inside is actually on the outside and vice versa. The person who is out of place is the version of self in the present. The past and future endure, but the present is static and uninhabitable. Perhaps the only reality not permissible is to live fully in the present.

'El ángel del baño' (The Angel in the Bathroom) presents a child who becomes enamoured of an angel she finds in her bathroom, or that she imagines is there. She tells her nanny, who regards it as a game. But is it? Is it an angel or an intruder? The man is hungry and dirty. He bathes and eats the food that the young girl gives him. A patrol arrives and arrests the man. Was the angel a vagabond? A guerrilla fighter? Or perhaps he really was an angel? 'God is going to punish you', she tells the patrol. As with the woman in 'Invitación', the child and the mysterious angel are off centre, outside the acceptable logic of the society. In 'Lázaro el buitre' (Lazarus the Buzzard), a buzzard likes to eat raw meat and has to be watched at funerals lest he eat the cadaver. Otherwise he is an accepted member of the community and gets around dressed and smiling. The first-person narrator is nevertheless wary as the buzzard took a peck out of his daughter's arm and ate his wife's dog. He takes the buzzard to the country one day to hunt and while it is flying, shoots it to the ground. When people comment that the buzzard no longer appears, the narrator tells them that he has probably left town the way he came, without warning or 'perhaps he had never existed, had never been in the town and he wasn't called Lazarus, but rather he had been a collective dream. As people stopped being concerned and forgot easily, I decided to do the same' (54). Is the buzzard a symbolic stand-in for a certain type of human being? Maybe. He likewise does not fully fit in this society and is at the mercy of others who will decide if he lives or dies.

In 'Melisa: juegos 1 al 5' (Melissa: Games 1to 5), a young girl rehearses several death and burial rituals as childhood games, firstly lying on the grass in the shape of a cross, much to the annoyance of her father, then mimicking in the hallway a dead cat run over by a car, and then in the kitchen a dead pigeon, which has fallen to earth and still has its eyes open. In the fourth game she covers her dolls faces in talcum powder to re-enact a funeral parlour. Her mother enters and apologizes for taking her to collect her grandmother's body. In the fifth game she is making figures of animals and food. Another tale of divided identity, this story could just as well be entitled 'Learning to Die'. What kind of society produces these kinds of childhood games? What are the child's emotions responding too? One suspects, as with other stories, a major traumatic societal event involving many deaths. What we have in all these stories is a distribution of bodies (especially mutilated ones) which does not fit state imperatives or 'acceptable' social imaginaries — bodies not in their proper places, emotions not in their proper places, a world out of joint.

Most of the stories in *De fronteras* possess this same enigmatic mix of the fantastic and the grotesque, the abject and the absurd, with death and violence as constants. In 'Hechos de un buen cuidadano (Part I)', (Actions by a Good citizen, Part I), the narrator arrives home to find an unexplained dead body in his kitchen. It's a woman's corpse:

> Lacerated. And it was fresh: the smell of the blood that remained was still mineral. The face was unknown to me, but the body reminded me of my mother's bony and prominent knees as if they did not belong to her, as if she had been lent them by another woman much taller and thinner than she. (17)

The narrator is impressed by the clean work of the murderer and after looking at the corpse more closely, decides that 'if it had the face of someone, she would be called Livid', alluding to the discoloured aspect of the cadaver's appearance. From here the story takes an even more surreal turn: instead of consternation or disgust at the presence of the unknown body, the protagonist maintains his composure and 'like any good citizen,' (17) places an ad in a newspaper alerting the potential owner of the corpse as to its whereabouts:

> Looking for the owner of a young girl's
> meaty corpse with knobby knees
> and a face like a Livid.
> It was abandoned in my kitchen, very close to
> the refrigerator, wounded and almost empty of blood.
> For information call: 271-0122. (17)

Humour and horror co-habit. Several people call to congratulate the man on his good citizenly deed, even a couple looking for their daughter, who seems to fit the description and the name of the body, but who 'should be alive, not dead' (18). The corpse is eventually given to a man looking for a male body, but who figures any corpse will do for a burial to pacify his family. One instantly sees the symbolic value of the story for a society whose empathy has been cauterized by collective psychological and emotional damage — every death, every body, is interchangeable in this novelistic environment. What is needed is merely an efficient, practical resolution for disposing of them.

'Hechos de un buen cuidadano (Part I)' might have ended there, but is reprised in Part II, as Hernández continues in Swiftian fashion. The narrator begins to receive lots of calls about the cadaver and since the issue of lost cadavers seems such a common occurrence, he sets up his home as a clearing-house for other corpses, complete with assistance from strangers who have the same problem. Together they place ads in the local papers. Eventually the process becomes carnivalized with food and drink being served and the practice becomes absorbed into daily routine, as it does in most of the stories. But when seven cadavers could not be identified and disappointed people were preparing to leave the house, the narrator relates his experience with Livid in order to raise their spirits. After they have gone, he chops the remaining cadavers into pieces, cooks them and feeds them to poor people. The reader is led to reflect on what kind of social space produces this kind of behaviour — obviously one that has been unable to appropriately process a catastrophic event. Nevertheless, these deaths must be processed in order to move on — they cannot be left to wander in limbo, symbolically or otherwise, so they become incorporated matter-of-factly into daily routines as a kind of failed act of mourning.

In 'Manual del hijo muerto' (Manual for Dead Sons), parents are given instructions on what to do with a dead son. The sub-heading of the story is more specific: 'When the son is in pieces'. Detailed instructions are given as if assembling or arranging the pieces of a model car or plane, including advice about having tissues on hand and not smoking during the process to avoid 'dampening or damaging with flame or ash the delicate pieces' (107). Instructions are given on how to identify a son's body by dental records if unsure. The text is accompanied by special commercial warnings set off in rectangular lines advising not to sign the delivery sheet for the box of body parts until you are sure they are the right ones because 'returns are not accepted' (107). Further detailed instructions are given about where best to assemble the body —'the dining room table'— (108) and once completed, how to mourn in the correct way. The macabre affect which issues from such description, as in other stories in the

114

collection, is not in the words themselves (no intensifying adjec-
tives reinforcing the horror of the description, no moralising), but
rather in the calculated, dispassionate way in which the instructions are narrated, as if this were a Nazi extermination camp
exercise in rational disposal of bodies. Here, affect registers in the
literary language by its absence — the not said. The affect created
by this absence, given the subject matter of the various plots,
imposes itself on the writing and reading process before any allegorical or theoretical meaning arrives. What lies behind the
production of dead bodies is left unexplained, as if that were old,
irrelevant news. The complete lack of affect in the language only
serves to intensify the affect summoned in the reading process:
the emotional reaction, and any ethical or moralistic position, is
left to the reader.

'Fauna de alcantarilla' (Sewage Fauna) presents us with a
nightmarish dehumanization of the subjects. A man lives in a
sewer with his wife and two children. He goes out three times a
day to get food for his family, hunting the cats and dogs that live
in the neighbourhood. The neighbours, alarmed by the situation,
ask the local watchman to catch him, however he escapes. They
plan to take him to the zoo, but he would not be accepted because
taking care of humans, based on past experiences, is very problematic and 'inconveniences the other animals' (64). Finally, they
decide to cover all the possible exits of the sewer and let the family
die of hunger and suffocation. After a week the local residents
decide to cover their bodies with lime so that the smell no longer
contaminates the neighbourhood. The story highlights not only
the precariousness of life for the poor, but the indifference of the
neighbourhood to the family's plight. This lack of empathy and
communication is fairly a constant theme in Hernández's short
stories— the absence of class solidarity where you would most
expect to see it. Neighbours and citizens in general view each
other with suspicion. These stories could be set in Colombia as
much as El Salvador. This transformation in the fortunes of the
most vulnerable would seem to have infused the lives of
everyone such that the father of the nameless family is described
by the narrator as 'slithering out of a sewer without clothes and
with scaly skin.' Reduced to the non-human, it is easier for the
people in the neighbourhood to request the family's extermination. One notes the total absence of not only compassion, but any
sort of state institution to intervene on the family's behalf.

In this world of strange characters and nightmarish scenarios, then, the macabre and the fantastic sit alongside the everyday and the mundane. But what is noticeable is the kind of distorted ethical framework that guides people's actions. Even though the stories are not without moments of tenderness or people performing mundane neighbourly routines — communicating, making cups of coffee for a stranger, taking biscuits and drink to an angel intruder, helping a stranger turn into an ox, and so forth — these people have had their moral compass distorted such that what should seem abhorrent seems like the practical thing to do. Many of the characters who carry out actions do so in seemingly the most rational, practical way, as if the situation called precisely for that sort of response. But here we need to park our moralism. Things are more complicated.

Yansi Pérez looks at the deeper meaning of how Hernández stages the restitution of a catastrophic loss through 'the grotesque presentation and radical metamorphosis of mourning' (Pérez 2014: n/p) in order to process, finalise, reverse or, as Pérez puts it, 'subvert' mourning. She identifies two ways that restitution is figured in Hernández's stories: through 'the protagonist attempts to mimic, to occupy the place of the lost cadaver' (Ibid.); or 'through a reincorporation of the cadaver into the world of the living' (ibid.). If in 'Manual del hijo muerto', an organisation mails dismembered parts of sons to their families for re-incorporation, in 'Abuelo' a dead grandfather is dug out of his grave and sawn into six pieces to be distributed to family members so that 'at family get-togethers, each person could take his part (no excuses) so that the grandfather would be complete' (Hernández 2007: 55). This 'literalization of mourning,' Pérez suggests, is just the reverse face of replacing the 'emotional, rhetorical, and political loss that the death of a loved one leaves' (Pérez 2014: n/p). But we need to try and understand what type of mourning is actually being processed, cancelled or subverted in the fictional construct itself. On the one hand, the stories symbolize or allegorize how, given a severe degree of trauma occasioned by a loss, people can be driven to gothic horror-like extremes of psychological and emotional reaction in order to cope: 'These stories propose a perverse fantasy of a mourning that only accepts total restitutions' (ibid.). But since that is impossible, except in the genre of the fantastic, how should we read these stories? Pérez identifies another way that mourning is processed — through the figuration of hospitality. In 'Hechos de un buen cuidadano (Part 1)', the bodies of unclaimed strangers are cooked and fed to poor people:

> How can one accept in one's own house that radical other, the cadaver of someone we do not know? How are we able to put this cadaver in circulation so that it can function in the economy (affective and material) of the living? This ethics of hospitality goes to the absurd extreme of offering as a gift, as food, this cadaver of a stranger to the homeless, to those whom nobody has given any hospitality. (Pérez 2014, n/p)

But is it really that extreme and absurd? This is also a Christic image of sacrifice — the body is sanctified by being consumed and vice versa, forging community bonds (except here it is literalized); in endo-cannibalism, the flesh or bone of someone belonging to the same community is consumed as a way of absorbing their spirit or showing respect, a practice identified in different places around the world, including in some tribes in Latin America. The dead are incorporated into the community for eternity. Seen in this light, the stories are less unimaginable than in Catholicism, for example, in which such practices are sinful and idolatrous.

Be that as it may, most critics read the short stories politically and interpret the fictional scenarios as allegories of El Salvador's civil war and its aftermath. Some even want to extend the causes to the neoliberalization of Central American economies in the wake of the peace accords (Kokotovic, A. P. Rodríguez, Cortez). But the stories are much more than this. An analysis of how mourning in 'Carretera sin buey' is staged might yield an answer if we approach it from the perspective of the status of the ox in the story. No mention is made or even insinuated as to the connection of the ox to the man or the community. We could imagine that including this story in the collection alongside ones that deal with human loss, is not just highlighting a process of dehumanization — the approach of Cortez, Pérez, Ortiz Wallner, Kokotovic, Jossa—but also highlighting an animal death that needs to be restored or redeemed somehow. And here I depart from the critics who want to concentrate on the supposed message about the denigration of human life, and focus, rather, on the status of the ox. In her analysis of 'Melissa: juegos 1 al 5', Emanuela Jossa refers to the final game in this way: 'Even this

117

activity, the most innocent, could be related to the death that obsesses Melissa: is the transformation of the animals in food not done perhaps through another crime?' (Jossa 2014: 23). Jossa does not pursue this point about the violence done to animals. However, the idea is suggestive, so let us develop it in 'Carretera sin buey'.

The story begins innocently enough with a couple travelling in their car in the countryside. They suddenly coming across what seems to be an animal on all fours 'looking towards the edge of the horizon' (Hernández 2007: 23).They soon realise it is a man. One of the couple is the narrator. Upon realizing their mistake, he or she declares: 'If we had known that it was a human being, we would not have stopped the car. We wouldn't have slowed down' (23). They really only stopped because they like animals. We soon find out that the man mistaken for an animal has accidentally run into an ox with his car on a bend in the road out of town, killing and later burying it as if it were human. He subsequently feels tremendous remorse for the absence/death of the ox and decides to 'take its place.' (24) He changes his appearance, gets on all fours, and even goes to the extreme of getting the two passersby to help castrate him. Both the man and the passersby agree that the result is successful, though the man still does not quite look like an ox because he lacks the dullness in his eyes, something that he appears unable to achieve. As the story ends, the narrator muses: 'It will take him a long time to dull his gaze' (25). Perhaps if the man had been castrated against his will, like the ox, his gaze would have dulled.

Critics want to read 'Carretera sin buey' as a metaphor or allegory for the legacy of political violence in El Salvador and how middle-class people find animals of more concern than humans, indicative of the state of values in the country post-civil war. Beatriz Cortez, for example, reads the story as a comment on those on the margins of 'cultural legibility' and frames her discussion in terms of identity. She regards the story as a metaphor for the way the *testimonio* genre was read by metropolitan centres in establishing marginalized identities (Cortez 2010: 155). Furthermore, the ox 'has a higher level of importance than the life of a human being . . . the ox can be interpreted as the fixed version of identity. The human life and liberty that the man has through his transformative possibilities must be sacrificed once the ox is destroyed' (156). She concludes that 'not only does the man detain his own act of self-transformation in order to perform the fixed identity of the ox, it is worse: he does it . . . from the definition of those who occupy the space of power' (158).

Cortez's interpretation is interesting and creative, but I am not persuaded because I think the extrapolations are too sociological and political in a story that, as in others by Hernández, gives no historical referents or locative cues to draw such specific sociocultural interpretations. It is an over-reading. It may in fact be more worthwhile to read the story against the grain of identity politics and see it as a theatrical staging of the unbreachable boundary between human and non-human species. This raises the key philosophical question of whether animals can be constructed as moral subjects and how we justify that. We need a more literal reading. This may not concord with authorial intention, but in no way is the reader bound by that, even if we could safely deduce it or if Hernández were to clearly lay out what she was trying to do. We therefore have at least two possible interpretative paths: try to divine authorial intention from the material textuality itself and paraphrase and allegorize it (the most common approach to the story); or while acknowledging the presence of authorial intention in the text, use the text as a point of departure for an eco-critical discussion.

The critics don't seem to pay much attention to the ox, preferring to locate the philosophical drama and the moral question in the attitude of the tourists towards animals rather than the man. But the most interesting staging is the struggle of the man to become animal. Indeed, it is the central axis of the story: the man feels a deep sense of pity and responsibility for the ox when it dies. Nevertheless, his attempt to 'save nature' founders on the unbridgeable gap between our rational consciousness and the non-human animal world. What is significant is the desire to make reparations, the empathy displayed by the man. Critics are silent on this because they are only looking for a political reading which reflects the state of human rights and social justice in Central America. But the construction of reality is the work of both human and non-human actors, all of whom have agency in that construction. They form the networks that make the world work ecologically. Yet we don't grant equal ontological status to non-human entities or categorise them as moral subjects. In the discussion of Rodrigo Rey Rosa's story 'Gracia' I referred to how Derrida has called for the deconstruction of this divide, this *fron-*

tera. Following Derrida, Dierdra Reber calls for a 'new vision' in which humanity 'humbly takes its place alongside every other species . . . instead of claiming sovereign exception' (Reber 2016:179):

> Derrida revisits the question of the radical frontier with the Other interrogated in decades past as being between races, genders, social classes, or ideologies — but always as intrahuman Otherness — and re-locates Otherness at the boundary between the species , between humans and animals . . . the Other poses the consummate moral challenge: knowing that the self-Other divide is untraversable, the self must yet attempt to traverse it for the sake of establishing a horizontal understanding that works to counter repressive hierarchies of power. (180)

It is here that Hernández's other stories unite with 'Carretera sin buey' in their coded critique of power structures of violence. We thus have two sides to an existential problematic: on one hand, a human animal with a highly developed rationality capable of abstract thought, but also with a range of emotions and feelings, including guilt; and on the other, a non-human animal, the ox, which is indifferent to humans' desire to overcome guilt for acts of violence against nature.

The sides cannot meet in a space of resolution: the rationalising, guilt-inducing subjectivity of the man is limited by the mute speech of the ox — the ox cannot inhabit our thought processes or feelings and dies in uncomprehending stupefaction towards its own suffering after being run into by the man's car, his technological prosthesis. Human beings are thus caught in this philosophical empty space in which we realise the damage we are doing to the non-human species and their habitat, but the non-human species are not capable of resisting our relentless onslaught with rational counter-actions. They are trapped within the limits of their species being and are but uncomprehending witnesses (and victims) to the destruction we have wrought. For Dipesh Chakrabarty:

> our political and justice-related thinking remains very human-focused. We still do not know how to think conceptually—politically or in accordance with theories of justice—about justice towards nonhuman forms of life . . . theo-

ries are limited by strict requirements relating to the threshold of sentience in animals. (Chakrabarty 2016: 110)

How might we establish the conditions, then, under which non-human animals becomes moral subjects with rights? Traditionally discourse focused on animal rights has appealed to the similarities between humans and non-humans based on certain properties that measure the degree of closeness of certain animals to us, including empathy, the ability to feel pain and to communicate in a rudimentary way with humans. For Michal Piekarski, the question cannot be sustained by appeals to animal 'properties'. The question of animal ethics must be posed as a transcendental question: 'What kind of ethics can include in its reflections both man and (other) animals?' (708). But human ethics is restricted to those who can speak or communicate with us in a way we can understand. We only offer

concern, responsibility, care and protection to those who are close to us. The animal is the remote Other which cannot be included in our 'rational' ethics of speaking beings. It seems that, contrary to what Levinas thought, Alain Badiou was right saying that we only recognise the otherness of the Other when he resembles us. (712)

Piekarski believes the answer therefore lies not in an ethics of speaking beings and questions of animals' nearness to humans, but in an 'ethics of commitment.' (713) He sees two ways of addressing the issue, both practical: one is material and technological — 'changing our existing practices of relating to animals,' (713) for example, by not eating meat; and the other is making a commitment, which involves responsibility: 'commitment changes the nature of our practices because it "feeds back" into itself. Being committed to the Other, I also become committed to myself' (713–14). For Pietkarski, in the ethics of commitment, it should not matter whether the Other is human or non-human: 'I respect you, I care for you and do not abuse you because I want or feel the need to be a better person . . . Commitment precedes ethics and makes it possible' (714). But where, then, do we draw the dividing line of respect? Let us imagine a continuum, a gradation of sentient beings: where does 'the animal' begin and end? We feel an affinity with simians, pets and dolphins, but are we going to respect the bull and not castrate it? And what about rats, to use a more extreme example? Piekarski does not resolve the problem, but the question he raises is necessary: under what conditions can an animal be a moral subject, that is, a subject of rights? We have come full circle to the position arrived at in our discussion of Rey Rosa's 'Gracia' in Chapter 4: in the absence of God, the ethical decision is in our hands as both readers and actors in real life.

8

Love and Sex in Times of Disenchantment
Reading Jacinta Escudos

'Sometimes I feel like a demon and others as clean as the Virgin Mary.'

EL DESENCANTO, JACINTA ESCUDOS

JACINTA ESCUDOS is a Salvadoran fiction writer whose writing project spans more than 30 years, and shows no sign of slowing down. She is the author of *Apuntes de una historia de amor que no fue* (1987), *Contra-corriente*(1993), *Cuentos sucios*(1997), *El desencanto* (2001), *Felicidad doméstica y otras cosas aterradoras* (2002), *A-B-Sudario* (2003), *El Diablo sabe mi nombre* (2008), *Crónicas para sentimentales* (2010) and *El asesino melancólico* (2015).

The two books chosen for analysis here are *Cuentos sucios* (Filthy Stories) and *El desencanto* (Disenchantment), though the themes highlighted recur in most of her literature: the disappointments of love between men and women, dysfunctional parenthood, the exploration of female sexuality and the deconstruction of female gender conditionings. The overall affect that issues from these fictions is not only disenchantment, but solitude. *Cuentos sucios* is a collection of eight stories from 8 to 20 pages long dealing with fantasies of psychological-sexual games and manoeuvres. Many of the themes will re-appear in *El desencanto*, the main focus of this chapter. *Cuentos sucios* is an experimental narrative on sexuality in scenes of betrayal, sadomasochism, onanism, voyeurism, a sexuality which appears to feed off the social emptiness and desolation reflected in a sombre landscape and the tensions existing in the surrounding society, alluded to in narrative or character asides. A man is shaving in his bathroom in the morning when he is suddenly surprised by a strange woman who has come in through the bathroom window. They enter into a linguistic game, but can't set the appropriate rules: 'The game consists in not believing anything of what others tell you, because in the end, they also play their own games' (12). The chance encounter leads to nothing as they have both found each other too late and cannot establish mutually agreed rules of engagement. In another story, a woman is in bed with a stomach ache when her anxious, paranoid lover arrives with stories of 'secret police who are loose all over the city, disfiguring with knives the faces of all those who worked with them so that their victims can't recognize them during war crime trials' (21). He lies down with her and begins to make love only to discover what he thinks is a different woman to the faithful Penelope he loves:

> She suddenly feels a whiplash of fire and something wet on her right cheek, she opens her eyes to discover the edge of a knife millimetres from her nose, the bright steel tinged with blood and a twisted grimace on Dante's mouth, a grin that looks like a smile, and the man's tongue brushing her cheek, licking her blood and floating in the air of his mouth like an atrophied octopus tentacle. (Escudos 1997: 24)

The mixture of sexuality, violence and horror parallels the society in which the two lovers move.

In the third story, 'Costumbres pre-matrimoniales', (Pre-Marital Customs), Claudio likes to invite his lovers to share his bed with his mother so she can listen to their love-making. It's her link to the past and keeps her young. After one such might, the young woman enters the kitchen in the morning and chats with the mother. The young woman has slept well: 'Yes, they all say the same', says the mother. 'And I listen while you make love. I feel revived and it makes me recall the good times way back when. Tell me: don't I look rejuvenated this morning?' (31). There is an obvious wink here, taken to hyperbolic lengths, to the often over-bearing presence of parents in their children's adult lives, even their sex lives. In '¿Y ese pequeño rasguño en tu mejilla?'

(And That Little Scratch on Your Cheek?), the narrator is involved in a love triangle with her boyfriend and her mother. The mother's betrayal is portrayed as consistent with her profile as a bad mother who abandoned her and her brother when they were little, only to eventually return to her father but then steal her boyfriend. Upon discovering the betrayal, the daughter locks the mother in the basement: 'It's a question of loyalties mum. Don't you understand? There are unshakable rules and this is one of them: the mother *never* takes the daughter's boyfriend' (43). Mothers and the 'maternal function' are often positioned as negative in Escudos narratives, unwelcome presences which inflect young people's decision making in perverse or negative ways. What is of note here is not so much the mother's transgression, as the fact that she *does* transgress, breaking the taboo of the abnegated, altruistic mother (this theme is taken up more fully in the final chapter).[36]

The fifth story relates a lesbian love that Annabelle feels for her childhood friend, Pina, now married to a man. Annabelle sends Pina love letters as if they were from a man. Pina gets used to them and anxiously awaits when the next missive does not arrive. Annabelle pays a man to go in her place for the first sexual encounter and film it. Pina thinks she is going to fulfil her fantasies with her secret admirer, and in a way she does, but she doesn't realize that she is also fulfilling someone else's desire. Annabelle proceeds to blackmail Pina. The game of homoerotic power and voyeurism allows Annabelle to vicariously possess Pina: 'Now I know you, naked, with a man, just as I wanted. Now I know the intensity of your screams when you have an orgasm. Now I know what pleasure looks like on your face' (59).

The sixth story is a surreal, oneiric fantasy which begins with the protagonist, a prostitute, raped on a street in Cuba. There is news of an elephant escaped from the zoo, three black dogs in a kitchen, a journal of dreams and a final scene of despair and suicide by poisoning. It is the most avantgarde of the collection and perhaps the least successful. In the seventh story, a cabaret dancer feels the power of her sexuality over the lascivious men watching her, and in the final story, 'The Night of the Murderous Writers', a male and female writer duel it out. Both are ex-guerrilla fighters now working at the same newspaper. As with other stories of Escudos, the female protagonist feels disgust with the sexual act, while the man defines himself and his sexual prowess through the size of his penis. The love-hate relationship between them is fuelled by writer's envy, punctuated by philosophical asides by the female about the difficulties of writing in the country they are from and the nature of writing itself: 'I do not believe in feminine or masculine literature. I think there is good or bad literature, regardless of the type of genitals the writer has in his/her crotch' (102–3). In a high stakes game of point-counterpoint and as the story draws to a close, we come to realize that the male protagonist, Boris, has been constructing the story from inside a prison cell after killing the woman, Rosanna. He tells a fellow inmate that he killed Rossana in self-defence. However, after he is released, in a final twist worthy of Cortázar or Borges, Boris decides to step out of his apartment to buy cigarettes, only to find Rosanna waiting for him. She shoots and kills him: 'And the story ends' (123). Yajaira Padilla reads the ending this way: 'Finally, Rossana's story or version of events is liberated. Ironically, what Rossana cannot achieve with her pen because there is no space for her in a male-dominated sphere she must achieve with a revolver, a token of the war and their previous existence together' (142).[37] This is a very suggestive and cogent reading. I read it in a related, but also metonymic level outside the fictional construct, and this goes to the very heart of post-war fiction and indeed this book: it is not the fictional shooting but Escudos' writing project itself, along with the later *El desencanto*, which occasions a symbolic rupture and begins to 'shoot down' the patriarchal domination of Central American letters (or at least causes it to tremble). The gendered pen which brings down the phallic sword.

If *Cuentos sucios* opens a literary space for more intimate, gendered narratives of female agency, *El desencanto* (Disenchantment, 2001) uses this space to explore more deeply the micro-negotiations of sexuality and love between heterosexual couples. Like *Cuentos sucios*, the novel allows us to reflect on female fantasy within the text as indicative of the ambivalence women feel towards love, sexuality, motherhood and relationships with men in a patriarchal world, especially when women are conflated with their vaginas. Here, the body is central, with all its libidinous desires, anxieties, pleasures, fears and attractions, an active agent in its own right. What Escudos' novel offers is a verisimilar portrait of a series of erotic encounters between a young female adult and a series of men. These encounters are not merely physical but fully affective and intersubjective: we are all affected in our intersubjective encounters with others, but sexual contact and feelings of love are perhaps the most heightened examples and also the most fraught. Such encounters leave us transformed, one way or the other. In the protagonist's case, youthful naivety is transformed into disenchantment and cynicism. *El desencanto* is a novel composed of 30 vignettes or episodes in a young woman's sentimental education between the ages of 19 and 35. Through her encounters with a variety of men, as well as her perceptions of what a woman is supposed to be according to society's normative standards, her amorous adventures underscore how women internalize male views of themselves and other women. Some episodes deal directly with sexual encounters, others with fantasies, others with reflections on the condition of women. The episodes involve consensual and non-consensual sexual experiences. For Ortiz Wallner, the date of the novel's publication, 2001, links the novel 'to a whole sensibility beginning to be represented by Central American narrative — disenchantment' (Ortiz Wallner 2102: 126). In fact *El desencanto*, along with Horacio Castellanos Moya's *El asco* (Revulsion, 1997), are two of the novels, more than any others, that signal a definitive break with the heroic dominant narratives of the revolution and its aftermath. But Escudos' novel stands apart for its ability to establish a realm of affect that steers clear of a didactic critical position in favour of rupture and ambiguity. The narrator presents the reality of the protagonist's sexual encounters in a crude, graphic way, without decoration or palliatives, even with a certain coldness. The protagonist's world may be disenchanted, but not so Escudos' fictional project, underpinned by its jagged sexual politics.

Arcadia, the protagonist on whom is centred all the action and feelings, is not so much an organic compositional unity as a name and a body linked to heterogeneous emotions and affect, registered in solitude and in intersubjective encounters through sexual activity. Arcadia is at least two people in one. But we are not talking of a split personality in need of psychoanalytical counsel, but rather two overlapping modes of being, one in search of a conventional notion of amorous encounter, and one bent on experimentation and sexual fantasy. This split is established through the juxtaposition of a third-person, omniscient narrator and Arcadia. The split is established from the beginning, before the first episode, with a quotation from a woman in her notebook, followed by the narrator's objective observation:

> *There are people who are afraid to speak about things. I hope I'm not afraid to speak about mine.*
> Thus the woman writes in her notebook and writes no more. She leaves the two phrases there while she leans back in her chair. She lights a cigarette. She thinks. (Escudos 1997: 9)

In the first experience, a chapter of barely four pages, 'El hombre que tiene manos de mujer' (The Man With a Woman's Hands), the narrator tells us that Arcadia is a nineteen-year old virgin who has never had a boyfriend. She meets a 40-something man who is remarkable for his beautifully maintained finger nails, though the rest of his physical aspect is decidedly unattractive. In the woods the man suddenly decides to kiss her. Focalization is through Arcadia's sensations. She feels a certain repulsion: 'I am put off by his moustache' (140). But she lets him kiss her anyway, keeping her eyes open the whole time, looking at the man's face. Focalization moves out to the narrator: 'But Arcadia is not there. She's not in those lips, in that kiss. She arrives at the forced, necessary conclusion, that between what bodies do and feelings, there is no true, narrow, absolute relation' (14). He then presses his body to hers and she lets him, briefly, though she remains 'rigid as a pole' (14). When the man becomes sexually aroused, she pushes him away saying that someone might see them, though we are told by the narrator that she is really worried of the shame of being seen with such an unattractive man. Things go no further. On another occasion, when they are returning home from an outing in his car, the man tries another advance going so far as to fondle her breasts and put his hand between her legs: 'Again she lets him do it, but without feeling anything' (14). The narrator informs us that she allows the man's advances because:

> she doesn't know how to say no. Nobody has spoken to her about such things. Nobody has told her about men, the things that they do when alone with women, about what women should do in such occasions. No female friend has confided to her this type of intimacy. Neither has her mother. (14)

She only knows an idealized version of intimacy learned through popular media — movies, books, songs. She feels no emotion for this man, or any man, and 'she doesn't understand (perhaps, ultimately, she never will), what a body has to do with love, if love is a feeling and the body is just material' (15). She puts up with his touching and him putting his tongue in her ear, which disgusts her, but she doesn't want to appear 'impolite, rude' (15). He places her hand on his penis. The narrator tells us that she has seen penises before when secretly leafing through pornographic magazines in kiosks, curious about what they look like in case 'one day she really sees one' (16). He forces her head down onto his penis and asks her to kiss it, even though it has 'an acidic smell of urine and sweat' (16). The man obliges her to perform *fellatio* and moans, while she only feels increasing revulsion. When he has an orgasm: 'The man kisses her cheek. She feigns a smile, but feels sadness. She doesn't know what to say to this stranger for whom she feels a profound disgust. She wants to open the car door and run. Her mouth feels dirty' (17).

Arcadia's stance is one of partial detachment towards her own body and her actions, especially sexual activity, as if she sees herself from the outside. How to interpret this? We need to move slowly here. We have only traversed the first episode/chapter of Arcadia's sentimental education. She is obviously portrayed as naïve and confused and masculine entitlement is on full display. Furthermore, he is an older man preying on a younger woman and taking advantage of her naivety and vulnerability. It is of little value, then, condemning the obvious — many men are like this and any sensitive reader would be appalled. What is more interesting, however, is the way the narrative is constructed such that the omniscient narrator focalizes the events through Arcadia's feelings and bodily reactions, but without passing moralistic judgment (which is reserved for the reader).Who is this narrator? What is her (we assume it is a female) function besides narrating? What is the affect created in reading and for whom? What affect would be created by a female reader activating the text compared to a man? Or are there a range of possible reactions in both male and female readers? Let's read on and see if we can be a bit more specific.

In the following chapter, 'El hombre de la primera vez' (The First-Time Man), a much longer thirteen pages, the narrator portrays Arcadia and all women as dreaming of the arrival of a 'Blue

Prince' on a white horse with blue blood, but then says: 'The colour of the horse and the blood are unimportant details for Arcadia, and it's not even important if he is a prince. It would be enough that he loved her' (21). This is a strong narrative intervention. By creating the fantasy visual image, but then saying Arcadia doesn't care about the details, means that the fantasy is the narrator's and we start to get a sense of the narrator's profile. Is it an older and wiser Arcadia noting down all her experiences? We suspect so, but until now we could not really speculate. The narrator continues with her mocking irony, but now in a discourse fit for a pop relationship counsellor or a five-cent manual for courting: 'It is also rumoured that if the said female person does not have her eyes open and her heart suitably disposed, the subject in question may pass fully and inadvertently through the jungle of sentiments, this constituting a tragedy of incalculable proportions' (21). The narrator, warming to the task, sees love as a roulette wheel or a game of poker and turns even more sarcastic, even regretful: 'try, try, try and never stop playing, until you win the prize or lose everything you gambled' (21). The narrator thus sets the mood for the loss of Arcadia's virginity which will come: 'It is in this mood that we find our dear protagonist seated on the Berlin metro . . . which in those days was divided by the wall (fondly remembered)' (22). The narrator was thus in Berlin then too. We can now establish that the narrator is indeed the chastened Arcadia at a much later date.

There is a certain faux voyeurism in all this, as the reader leans in more closely trying to predict what Arcadia's next adventure will be and how she will react. Her mood is described as a mixture of apprehension and modest excitement, a feeling of being drawn to a risky rendezvous with a man twenty years her senior. She reflects on losing one's virginity as no big deal. Nevertheless, the narrator sets up the scene as Little Red Riding Hood and the wolf. When Arcadia asks about a wall they are passing by, focalization shifts rapidly between the narrator, the consciousness of the 'wolf man' and Arcadia:

> He thinks of answering her with 'it's the wall where I will corner you and rip your clothes off, all the better to eat you, my dear Red Riding Hood', but settles for a conventional: 'It's a cemetery'. Ah, how romantic, thinks Red Riding Hood, walking with the ferocious Wolf next to the wall of a cemetery on a starry night

heading towards the slaughter yard: Red Riding Hood in the sky
with neon lights. (24)

Once at the wolf's apartment, Arcadia is encouraged to remove
her clothes as the narrator continues with the Red Riding Hood
sexual fantasy. They get under the sheets and the man lies on top
of her, Arcadia finds it harder to breath with his weight on top
and muses on the disjunction between what is happening and
what she was led to expect, her mind full of pop cultural representations and myths of romance: 'there should have been a
dinner with wine and candles, a box of chocolates and a bunch of
flowers, endless prior phone calls, perfumed letters and a count-
less number of sugary words whispered in her ear, all
accompanied by little bells and violins' (27). Arcadia waits for the
moment when her body suddenly 'clicks' and she feels an over-
whelming desire and is 'transported to the interstellar regions of
pleasure and all that blah, blah, blah that she has heard about sex'
(28). When the wolf man finally enters her, she recalls all the
conventional societal advice about 'the first time' and the sacred-
ness of the act and the bond that is supposed to be forged, but
none of this occurs.[38] She unromantically describes the initial
sensation of being entered to stuffing a dry tampon in her vagina
and her mind wanders to periods and what table top dancers do
when they are menstruating because:

> the bosses of those bars are usually fat guys, bearded and with a
> stinky cigarette stuck in their mouth, they couldn't understand
> the poor girls that arrive one day with terrible abdominal pains
> and request a day off so that . . .
> Suddenly her reflections are interrupted by a military order-
> shout from Wolf:
> 'Move!', said in a tone that to Arcadia seemed not the least
> romantic nor even sympathetic. (29)

Wolf realizes she is a virgin and gets annoyed and tries to move
her himself by grabbing her hips. All of this seems comical to
Arcadia who nevertheless 'desires something to happen or that
it end soon, because it all has her, frankly, bored' (30). The narrator enters Wolf's mind again through free indirect discourse in
order to mock his insecurities as he transforms from 'an astro-
naut' into just an ordinary wolf disguised again as the

131

grandmother and waiting 'for all the red riding hoods who lose their way, ah, the little bitches, all easy to divert from their path, such easy game for wolfs and hunters, or what do you think, that the red riding hoods dress in red because that's the only colour in the store?' (31). The sexual act over, Arcadia is offered a cigarette because 'it's good when you haven't had an orgasm' (31), the wolf tells her. They chat and Arcadia is told off for not revealing she was a virgin. She gets dressed and leaves to walk back to the station, unaccompanied because 'he's really tired' (33). Arcadia walks alone in the cold night air thinking nothing else can happen to her now since a woman only has two things to lose: 'her virginity and her life' (33). She hides her gaze from her mother when she arrives home 'as mothers know when it's the first time' (33). She feels a sense of accomplishment and goes to bed 'happy to have another secret hidden from mum. Now they are both equal' (34). She sleeps with Wolf two more times and like the first, remains unsatisfied and bored and so consigns him to the past, and 'Red Riding Hood continues her path in the wood, walking, searching, hoping; that is to say, alone' (34). This graphic and thoroughly unromantic description of initiation into sex and its aftermath continues throughout the book.

In 'blá, blá, blá', two women discuss faking orgasms. 'Don't you think men know you are faking it?':

> I don't know . . . But the truth is the man is so absorbed in his own pleasure that he doesn't notice the difference. In the end they ask you if you enjoyed it. And you have to respond in the affirmative . . . if you say you had two orgasms, they will still ask if you are sure you didn't have three, because they felt three. (46)

This play of charades and masking is one we also identified both in *Managua Salsa City* and Hernández's stories. In one of the more intense scenes in 'Las ratas serán buenas madres para ti, hijo mío' (The Rats Will Be Good Mothers For You, My Son), Arcadia's period is late. She waits until something inside her body tells her that she is pregnant: 'The revulsion, the insuperable revulsion in the mornings and the total loss of appetite. A heavy, lethargic sensation in the body' (57). The body takes central stage, a character in its own right, the sheer materiality of the body. She decides to see a doctor:

It's the first time she has seen a gynaecologist in her life. It's the first time she has taken her clothes in front of a man that is not going to sleep with her. It's the first time she has had to mount on that contraption, worthy of the tortures of the Inquisition, in which she must adjust her feet, open her legs and have her genitalia open to the cold air of the surgery and the petrified gaze of the doctor, who advises her that the speculums he has are too big for her, but he'll have to use them anyway because there are no others. With particular brutality, the man accommodates them between Arcadia's vaginal labia as she shakes with the cold metal and the uncomfortableness of the pain and the infinite shame of that stranger practically sticking his nose in her intimate parts. (59)

The image is indeed one of torture. Like most of Arcadia's bodily experiences, it comes upon her as an unwelcome surprise, 'the worst tragedy in the world happening to her' (60). This is a far cry from the ideology of maternity that popular culture has sold her. According to Iris Marion Young, this alienation from the body is not uncommon in women:

the modalities of feminine bodily existence have their root in the fact that feminine existence experiences the body as a mere thing — a fragile thing, which must be picked up and coaxed into movement, a thing that exists as looked at and acted upon. To be sure, any lived body exists as a material thing as well as a transcending subject. For feminine bodily existence, however, the body is often lived as a thing that is other than it, a thing like other things in the world. (Young 2005, 39)

Either way, Arcadia has decided that the child will not be born: 'She doesn't want to be anybody's mum, doesn't want to be like her mother, ever' (61). She decides on an abortion. The father of the child tries to dissuade her, but his pleas are quickly dispatched. He resorts to the only pressure he knows that really gets to her — God: 'Arcadia believes in God, in sin, in eternal punishment' (62). But she goes ahead anyway. On a day of heavy rain and deserted streets and not having eaten, she arrives at the clinic with her boyfriend still trying to change her mind. The doctor informs her that the curettage will take an hour. She is anaesthetized, but wakes up while the operation is still going on: 'She feels the doctor poking around inside her and hears him throwing things in a metal bucket. She hears the sound of those invisible things striking the bucket. Then she notices the doctor get up and tip the contents of the bucket in the toilet bowl and pull the lever' (64). She imagines the foetus travelling down the pipes into the city sewer where it will live like a subterranean inhabitant until 'a rat eats it and it is mixed with all the shit from all the people in the city' (65). The doctor tells her to lie back and sleep, that all is going well, but he's not finished yet. She goes into a kind of fantasy delirium. When she wakes the doctor informs her that all is fine and she can go home and rest. As the scene ends:

> Outside it is raining, and continues raining. It rains the whole week.
> People die, the crops are drowned, houses crumble and the streets are flooded.
> 'National Tragedy', scream the newspaper headlines.
> She doesn't cry. She is unaware of anything. She just sleeps.
> The sleeping beauty of disaster. (69)

This kind of desolation is rarely novelized this way in Latin America and certainly not in Central America. It is meant to shock and be a corrective to societal fantasies about women and their reactions to sexuality, pregnancy and motherhood. It is a bleak portrait of the counter-face to the popular imagination. One imagines most men not only feeling squeamish faced with this narrative, but also feeling more than a little guilty as they peer into the mirror of their own comportment. How women react to the reading is for women to decide.

Further situations in Arcadia's sexual apprenticeship include an encounter with 'El hombre de las bofetadas' (The Man Who Likes to Slap), a lover who likes to slap his women while in the act. Arcadia meets a man at a bus stop and finds him quite attractive. Even though she feels a tinge of apprehension, she decides to go out with him. By this stage in her trajectory she is self-confident and enjoys the chase: 'She likes his smell, his saliva, his way of kissing, his hair, the night, the conspiracy against morality, challenging fear' (74). But this guy is strange: 'He hits her, he hits her a lot, but only in the face. And each time he does it he drives his member hard into her vagina. Arcadia looks at his ecstatic face, hears his uncontrollable moaning, absorbed in his pleasure' (78). Though she is not excited by the slaps, when she sees the man excited she enjoys the process. This story presents us with a dilemma. Arcadia seems to fail to comprehend the roots of her desire. Is it generated by her, or does she always take her cue from men? Should the reader condemn her, or is all fair among consenting adults? Feminists would find cold comfort in her passivity in face of male desire.

In 'El hombre que se equivocó' (The Man Who made a Mistake), the narrator is Arcadia herself as she relates in highly lyrical and allusive fashion a sexual encounter. She slowly builds up an image of total surrender: 'Taking off your clothes is taking off many masks. Allowing your skin to be touched is to place yourself at the mercy of death itself' (87). At the height of her passion she feels that the only plank on her sinking ship is the man's back: 'Save me', she whispers to him, but he 'mentions the name of another woman.' (88). The house of cards comes crashing down again. Another defeat. Another disappointment. 'Las listas' (The Lists) presents two women conversing about how many men they have slept with, even though they are only 25 years old. We assume one of them is Arcadia. They muse about why they do that, with so many: 'It's a search. We seek with urgency something we need. We are looking for love' (114).

The rest of the scenes/episodes in the book relate different male sexual fantasies that Arcadia must endure, some willingly. But at the end of her odyssey, her overall feeling is one of deception and disenchantment. Does Arcadia show any self-reflexivity or is she constitutionally incapable of learning from mistakes? Does she go through any kind of transformation other than a movement from naivety and innocence to disenchantment? Where does change come from? Escudos sets up her female character to highlight a process of subjectification and de-subjectification as she attempts to negotiate sexual and amorous encounters. The final self we are left to contemplate is certainly chastened and disenchanted, but she has not passed through her self-mourning and remains melancholic and disappointed. The book ends as it began with another first-person aside followed by third-person narrative comment — another novelistic ending without closure: '*Sometimes I feel like a demon and others as clean as the Virgin Mary*. That is the last phrase the woman writes in her notebook. She finishes her cigarette, gets up and turns off the light' (203).

For Beatriz Cortez in *La estética del cinismo* (The Aesthetics of Cynicism, 2010), *El desencanto* is emblematic of a more general cynicism in Central American literature because, in spite of the positive experience of exposing traditionalist morality, which makes women subservient to male desire and the male gaze, the novel nevertheless 'leaves us with a bad taste of broken promises: Arcadia, the protagonist, never experiences pleasure' (284). This is not completely true, since Arcadia experiences pleasure in sexual fantasy, but we take Cortez's point: the overall affect from start to finish is one of resignation and disenchantment. Arcadia is not capable of passing all the way through her dejection. But there is no reason why she should have to. Fiction's role is not to offer activist readings. Cortez claims that it is also 'perturbing to realize that the narrator also expresses her position in accord with Arcadia's' (289) by opining that Arcadia's dream of an idealized 'blue prince' arriving to whisk her way is consistent with girls and women of all ages, 'that I know' (21, cited in Cortez, 290). But this in no way means the narrator assumes the same ideology as Arcadia. In fact, the separation of the narrative voice of the older, chastened Arcadia seems to be precisely to highlight her inability to transform. But that does not make either the narrator or Escudos text 'cynical' or conservative or indeed 'disenchanted'. For what Cortez does is more or less direct a charge of nihilism against Escudos, the novelist, and collapses the distance between the fictional scenario and the author's purported values and intentions. Magdalena Perkowska has also identified this slippage between art and politics. She refers to an interview with Franz Galich in which the novelist points out that 'even though it [contemporary Central American fiction] is a literature in which the characters are cynical, it is not a literature of cynicism, and it's not a literature in which we express a total and profound disenchantment for a lack of utopias and perspectives' (Galich quoted in Perkowska 2011: 5). Perkowska underlines 'the fundamental difference between cynicism of the characters in Central American fiction and the supposed cynicism of the literature itself' (6), a distinction which, for Perkowska, is collapsed in concepts like the aesthetics of cynicism. She adds that, anyway, there still persists 'different forms of latent utopianism' (7) in this fiction. I could not agree more. Leaving behind direct political-ideological commitment in literature does not evacuate aesthetic and ethical commitment. We might also refer to Sara Ahmed here. In a different context, and in relation to women's literature, Ahmed takes issue with this way of seeing such novels:

> We need to question what is appealing in the appeal to happiness and good feeling . . . some critics suggest that we have paid too much attention to melancholia, suffering, and injury and that we need to be more affirmative . . . that presumes that bad feelings are backward and conservative and good feelings are forward and progressive. Bad feelings are seen as orientated toward the past, as a kind of stubbornness that 'stops' the subject from embracing the future. Good feelings are associated here with moving up and getting out. [But a] concern with histories that hurt is not a backward orientation: to move on, you must make this return. (Ahmed 2010: 50)

Arcadia's accounts of her sexual experiences are thick with affect, peppered with intimations of violence and exploitation, and linked by Escudos in complex ways: pleasure and pain, enjoyment and disgust, attraction and repulsion — gender aesthetics at its most entangled. *El desencanto* offers a politics of the body, of touch, of the desiring gaze as much as a vehicle for exposing the horrors of bad or unsatisfying sexual encounters. Intimacy is precarious in this sometimes sordid, pessimistic and sad world. Arcadia performs an operation of de-identification with the female role society expects her to play. She displays psychological strategies of displacement and sublimation in order to mitigate the intolerable, yet is fatally drawn to the encounters. Is Escudos offering us a sensual and sexual pedagogy? Maybe. She presents a complication for feminist stances: her female characters — certainly Arcadia — are rightly disgusted and disillusioned with heterosexual men, but they are also at times knowingly complicit with their own disillusion, choosing the path of risk and experimentation with men who they have only briefly met. Arcadia lacks a compass. We are tempted to categorise her as a borderline masochist. In other words, a simple feminist denunciation of the psychological defects and predictable ineptness and egotism of many men in their sexual and emotional relations with women must deal with the edge that Escudos works, that blurred border between revulsion and attraction that her female characters display towards predatory, self-centred and often cruel men and their sexual desire — her characters willingly go towards their own exploitation or humiliation, presumably because this also opens the possibility that the right partner might eventually be found. There are echoes here of Lars von Trier's controversial film, *Breaking the Waves* (1996), and the 1996 *The Vagina Monologues;*[39] so too the 'sex-positive' debate in feminism.[40] Some scenes in *El desencanto* would constitute rape — men forcing themselves on women. But Escudos' fictional sexual events, if they were to be witnessed with no explanation (and Escudos plays with the gaze constantly), would miss the agency that Escudos' female characters exhibit. And this agency appears to accord, in part, with so-called sex-positive feminism, originally an outgrowth of a growing schism within feminism after the 1970s on the questions of pornography and prostitution, both considered by many feminists to be irredeemable instances of patriarchal control of sexuality, 'sexual liberalization as a trend that only increases male privilege' (Chang 2008: 269).

Whichever stance is taken towards Escudos' fiction, it does stage the freedom for women to assume their desires and fantasies: literature and fantasy as places in which women can experiment with and control their desire. It is important to note that Escudos writing is not a queer literature: her fictional women are generally heterosexual, unsatisfied, and contradictory in their desires and they have the right to be so. Arcadia is a Christian. As the narrator reminds us, she believes in God and sin. Within Christianity pleasure has a long tradition of being linked to guilt. This may go part of the way of explaining how her character is both attracted and repulsed by sexual activity. This religious dimension is not explored by Escudos, however. Either way, Escudos has stated publicly that she is neither a feminist writer nor a female writer — just a writer, period. What one admires about her fiction is its experimentalism — she transgresses in search of liminal fictional experiences which place both her characters and her readers in ambiguous moral and ethical situations. The sense of unease in reading Escudos' narrative is productive of meaning and we should see it this way rather than decry her portrayal of women wilfully drawn to their own degradation and disappointment in exploitative relationships. Just like her characters, Escudos takes risks and challenges the unwritten rules of both society and interpersonal relationships, sexual or otherwise, not knowing in advance the outcome. In Rancièrean terms, her literary politics lie in the undecidability of aesthetic experience, her ability to reorganize the distribution of the sensible, the way we see, feel and act in intimate situations. Didacticism would remove the perverse strangeness that shocks and titillates, but which also invites us to re-think how we relate to each other, especially men and women. Escudos opens up a broader space for literary experimentation for all Central American writers, not just women. *Cuentos sucios* and *El desencanto* have a kind of audacious, insolent beauty.

9

Chronicle of a Suicide Foretold
Denise Phé-Funchal's *Ana sonríe*

'How many times have people used a pen or paintbrush because they couldn't pull the trigger?'

VIRGINIA WOOLF

DENISE PHÉ-FUNCHAL (1977–) is a Guatemalan writer and sociologist. She has published the novel *Las Flores* (2007), a book of poetry, *Manual del Mundo Paraíso* (2010), a book of short stories, *Buenas Costumbres* (2011), a children's novel, *La habitación de la memoria* (2015) and the novel *Ana sonríe* (2015). Phé-Funchal belongs to the younger generation of writers born after 1975. Her short stories express violence and a dehumanized world through the fantastic and the surreal. In this her Central American precursors are Jacinta Escudos and Claudia Hernández. As in the previous chapter, where we looked at Jacinta Escudos' short stories collected in *Cuentos sucios* as a preamble to *El desencanto*, this chapter begins with a brief analysis of *Buenas costumbres* before moving to *Ana sonríe*.

Phé-Funchal first drew major attention with *Buenas costumbres* (Good Manners), a collection of short stories with themes of family relations and parental control, the violent father and the castrating mother, death, religion, unrequited love and eroticism, misogyny, all told with a touch of the fantastic and horror, irony with a grim smile, written from the viewpoint of the victim: the intense love between two brothers leads to the death of one of them; a religious fanatic experiences sexual fantasies; the fear of living in a house full of anthropomorphized cockroaches; a young woman's parents buy little children and leave them to fend for themselves like pets in the house; a man brutalised by his father-less upbringing kills his poverty-stricken mother and takes out his anxieties on his lover ('I had to hit you to shut you up, just like her') (Phé-Funchal 2011:66). 'Wheel' (*Rueda*) is narrated in first person through the consciousness of a man who has spent more than 30 years in a wheel chair. As a toddler, he had watched his father ('I think it was my dad') disappear in the distance down the tracks of the ravine at the end of their street, never to return. He and his mother are left in poverty. Since the child looks like his father, his mother obliges him to work and bring in money. The woman who lives next door comes up with a scheme: she rents a second-hand wheelchair to the mother and suggests she place her son in it in order to attract alms. The scheme is a success and henceforth the neighbour also receives modest payments for her usury. One day in the park, the child decides to stand up out of the wheelchair, potentially risking the business and prosecu-tion, so he is furiously beaten by the mother. The woman next door sees an opportunity and encourages the mother to tie the son to the chair and take him out in public with his bruises and distorted mouth and blame the beating on the absent father. She also suggests the mother avoid parks and so she places the son outside a supermarket. The deception works wonderfully well and the son continues to gather money. When the bruises begin to heal, however, the alms dry up. At the suggestion of the neigh-bour, the mother resorts to beating the child with a piece of wood to maintain his pitiful appearance. The artifice continues for many years and both mother and neighbour survive off the income. By this time the son is mute from the beatings, can no longer stand up and his skin is mottled and discoloured 'like the sky' from the beatings. Eventually, the mother ceases the subterfuge as the local people have become suspicious of the child's ongoing condition. As the story ends, the mother and the neighbour walk off into the distance towards the edge of the ravine, arguing 'like two buzzards' over who owns the chair after 30 years. Seated in the doorway of the house, the man remembers again his first steps as a toddler and his father's disappearance and sets his chair in motion down the hill, 'towards them, towards the ravine, towards the sky that looks like me' (13).

This small horror story, which is not beyond the bounds of the possible in real life, suggests several critical themes, including the wretched life of the poor in the region, especially children, the issue of absent fathers, and the deconstruction of motherhood. We are given no clues as to why the father left, but the mother's incessant crying suggests that it was not her who instigated the separation. This leaves the reader to conjecture about the responsibility of the father and the frequency of abandoned families. In fact the phenomenon is a typical scenario in Central America due to poverty, the need to pursue work wherever it is available and, of course, a macho culture that provides a context in which such behaviour flourishes. Whatever the causes insinuated in the story, however, the focus is squarely on forced child labour and torture as a response to poverty, made horrific by the child's mother being the perpetrator. But Phé-Funchal does not judge through her first-person narrator: though the reader is faced with the uncomfortable images of physical abuse and exploitation, there is no moral centre in the story, save that of the reader. Filial piety recurs in the story in the way that the man recalls his initial joy riding around the house in the chair and the way that he is not ceded judgement by the author: nowhere in the story does Phé-Funchal allow her character to directly criticise the actions of his mother or the woman next door or recriminate his absent father. In fact the character the author invites us to contemplate is, if not retarded, nevertheless so crushed in spirit that even his recollections are couched in the language of a child resigned to its fate. What is noticeable in the fiction of Phé-Funchal, then, as in that of two other writers in this volume, Carlos Cortés and Jacinta Escudos, is a lack of preaching — the reader herself can readily divine the core of the problem: unreconstructed masculinity and the ideology of motherhood, the latter a taboo virtually untouchable in public discourse in Latin America.

In 'Zapatos' (Shoes), shoes carry out a metonymic function for a rigid and domineering masculinity in a scene of repeated male spousal violence. Through free indirect discourse, looking back at his childhood and focalising events as if he were still that boy, a man displays the psychological wounds inflicted by inter-generationally transmitted masculine behaviours. The boy observes and internalises his father's routines and command-ments and how his mother was 'educated' by his father to be a 'good woman'. We are given insight into the rituals of a discipli-narian and his fastidious vanity: the correct presentation of pants, shoes and shirts and the organisation of the domestic interior taken to absurd and nightmarish lengths:

> Pants ironed and shirt starched. Shoes gleaming. The path full of puddles I avoid time and again. Seated during recess and eating with gloves. My nails. The nails of a man. His pants. Exercise books and the handwriting of a man. Integrity and cleanliness. Honour. Finger wiped across the table. Close inspection of the fold in the sheets. The woman of the sheets. The woman of the hearth cleaning since morning to the rhythm of my father's snoring. She moves through the house in silence, dusting away the sleepy particles before the anxious eyelids open. Mum never went out. I went to the shop. Mum never went out because at least once a week the dust was not vanquished on time . . . then she paid for it. He educated her and the wounds and the purple skin took charge of mum's body. (42)

As the story closes, the narrative voice adopts a sinister pose, as if directly addressing the reader: 'A man enjoys educating. Don't forget it. I don't want to have to educate you all over again' (43).

In 'Partiré manana' ('I'll Leave Tomorrow'), a woman is asphyxiated by domestic life and contemplates leaving her family, children and all. She seeks comfort for her alienation in solitary routines as she reflects on her husband:

> I like to get lost in books; in mine because yours do not exist. Your children play around me and call me mother. But I did not give birth, they simply left my body, they deposited their smiles on him, but they fed on me, they robbed my sleep, they kidnapped my dreams and the possibility of returning to the sea. (47)

The woman dreams that her bags await her, packed in the wardrobe: 'I dream I have had time to prepare everything, that this routine will not be repeated tomorrow, that I'll never have to answer you again, that I will return to the cliffs and the waves that shout with me as they break' (49). We sense as readers, however, that the woman's inertia will cause her to keep

143

repeating the routine. Numerous economic, social, cultural factors are suggested that prevent women from leaving abusive homes. Violence is often seen as a 'normal' pattern of behaviour across many cultures, a familiar pattern for both women and men. Men who abuse are rarely odious all the time, and can even display love and attentiveness (as we saw in Carlos Cortés's *Larga noche hacia mi madre*). But mostly women who live in abusive or broken relationships remain economically dependent on the abusive male partner and often have to weigh the spectre of living in poverty against the abuse.

In 'Chapstick', it is the mother's abuse that comes under the spotlight. A mother has been unable to properly mourn the death of one of her daughters, the most spoilt, the one she was grooming to be the perfect woman. She forces one of her remaining two children to act as substitute object for the idealized lost daughter, dressing her in the same clothes and getting her to adopt the same rituals, including following a strict diet, learning to be impeccable with the application of make-up and so forth. Phé-Funchal cleverly holds back the surprise until the end when the child enters the bathroom to urinate: 'I hear my mother cursing in the kitchen. I've got time. I can free myself from these damn panties that have my penis trapped and pee like a man' (58). The sudden revelation of a boy forcibly dressed as a girl jars the reader and calls forth a second reading to apprehend the damaged psychological state of the mother, who in her grief has been unable to overcome the traumatic loss.

In the eponymous 'Buenas costumbres' ('Good Manners'), a young woman's mother advises her on the ideal man for her future husband:

> He would be a tall, handsome man with blue eyes, white teeth, wide-breasted, long hands, thin feet, sensitive, romantic, with a future, perhaps an engineer, doctor or pastor ... Mum said that by twenty-five I should already have two years of marriage, a maid, at least one child, a dog, a good suitcase and not be paying rent. (73)

We hear echoes of Arcadia's Blue Prince. As the story advances, the ideal man does not arrive — the young woman's mother is progressively disappointed with the shortcomings of the suitors and their professions and summarily dismisses them all: 'Mum said that Manuel did not take care of me, that Andrés's was not a profession, that Marino was a Jew, Antonio was poor, that Miguel was a driver, that Augusto was very ugly, that Nicholas was an artist, that Daniel was a lawyer and that Alberto smelled like a faggot' (74). Desperate to comply with her mother's and society's expectations, at 30 years old the woman seeks out her former boyfriends and proceeds to kill them and store a composite of body parts — one part from each boyfriend— in a bathtub of ice. The brain is reserved for mother, however, since only 'she knows how my ideal man should conduct himself' (75).

These artistic sketches of problematic motherhood join a virtual chorus in recent Central American literature.[41] In 'Violence au féminin: Mères castratrices et filles assassins' (2017), Julie Marchio highlights the conflicted relationship between mothers and daughters in the literary works of Central American female writers and delineates a process of desacralization of the taboo figure of the mother in images of psychic and physical violence perpetrated by mothers against their children. In Hispanic societies motherhood is traditionally associated with the image of the Virgin Mary: 'Chastity and maternity are the two pillars of "Marianism"... a counterpart to "machismo" . . . based on the idealization of the supposed moral superiority of women who display self-abnegation and sacrifice towards children and spouses' (Marchio 2017: 3). In particular, Marchio looks at the way the mother is often constructed as capable of cruelty, aban-donment, controlling behaviour and jealousy and not just the Marian ideal of abnegation. The portrait that emerges is thus complex: mothers as faithful transmitters of patriarchal values, inculcating societal expectations in their children, but also mothers who exercise a kind of negative agency, dominating and policing their daughters' lives. The result in this fiction is recur-ring *topoi* of the orphaned daughter, the sexually liberated daughter, the castrating mother, the neurotic mother, the sexual-ized mother, the violent mother, and so forth. For Marchio, taking her lead from Barbara Dröscher's work on mother-daughter rela-tionships in Central American literature since the 1970s:

In all these narratives, the sudden break with the mother seems to be a necessary condition for the advent of a sexuality free of taboos . . . In other words, the death of the mother allows the protagonist to escape the repressive mechanisms of patriarchal society transmitted from generation to generation by women/mothers and contributes to the liberation of desire, desire to be fulfilled otherwise. If there is no direct demystification of the figure of the mother, which is often idealized in remembrance, these representations constitute a roundabout way of expressing the castrating role the mother plays with her daughter. (Marchio 2017: n/p)

Many of the themes addressed in *Buenas costumbres* reappear four years later in *Ana sonríe*: failed domestic relationships, disenchantment, family dysfunction, duplicitous males, and so forth, but without the horror of *Buenas costumbres* (save that of patriarchy itself). The novel is constructed as a series of interwoven descriptions of the daily routine and vicissitudes of three Guatemalan sisters — Ana, Loretta y Lucretia — during one twelve hour period leading up to Ana's suicide. Phé-Funchal unfolds the truth of the lives of these women through the rhythms and the minutiae of their mundane daily activities, a congeries of both chance and willed events. The story is controlled by one omniscient narrator whose voice often blends with the sisters' thoughts in free indirect discourse. The book is divided into 38 chapters, each composed of one long, unbroken paragraph. Thirty-six are evenly dedicated to the three sisters in three parallel streams of narration. They serve to reconstruct both individual and extended family stories, as well as that of another dozen more minor characters that play a part in their lives. The mathematical symmetry of the three sisters' individual journeys, each told through twelve affective snapshots, creates a feeling of compression, in spite of the leaps into the past through memory and dream. The progression is bookended by the scene of Ana's suicide at the very beginning and repeated in paraphrastic form at the very end. Narrated twice, it encapsulates the whole story in a structure of quasi-predestination and inexorability, as well as a single present moment rather than a concatenation of chronological events. It is left to the reader to draw causal connections as he/she sees fit since this present is spun from the memories, chance occurrences, fears and hopes expressed by each sister.

The scene of suicide resonates with themes of suicide and mutilation and the more general affect of resignation and disappointment identified in Escudos and Hernández fictional works. Central American readers might recognise the particular lower-middle class fraction portrayed in the novel and the subtle local cultural and spatial references. These form a certain idea of a city, though Phé-Funchal insists that it is not Guatemala City, presumably because this would send the reader too quickly to a sociological or political reading (Phé-Funchal 2015c: n/p). There is no direct reference to politics either, but what is referenced strongly is the fear of poverty and solitude. This is not a fictional society in which you want to be abandoned or without money. In fact one imagines a wholly different reading experience created by a 'local' reader with his/her own particular cultural, social and political configuration. The appraisal of the novel offered here can only gesture towards the much richer reading experience by such a cultural 'insider' capable of decoding the signs and testing the affect summoned in the reading process. Be that as it may, this novel also transcends the local by drawing attention as much to its structure, affect and narrative style as merely reproducing a recognizable Guatemalan experience.

The narration balances the individual preoccupations of each sister with their collective family unity. But it is the characters and not the narrator who orient the narrative through their cognitive and emotional perspectives. Phé-Funchal makes use of the all the modernist narrative techniques, including shifting foci, parallel stories and cinematic time shifts through each character's memory. The future tense is occasionally used to anticipate for the reader and to create a sense of both premonition and sense of self-inflicted fate. Dialogue is unmarked yet still present through free indirect discourse in the sisters' recollections. Each sister's trajectory could be followed separately by skipping to every third chapter to follow each without interruption (a second reading this way is rewarding), but the reader would lose the connectivity and the simultaneity of the narrative as it builds an affective space in which each sister responds in their own way to the social and familial context in which they process disappointment. The novel maintains an intense intimacy throughout, with the final chapter restating in alternative form Ana's vertiginous end. Why repeat the final scene of suicide at the beginning? What was Phé-Funchal striving for? One possible reason for having the suicide at both ends of the story may be to cut off any interpretation that might suggest things could have been otherwise in the beginning. Perhaps the author wants us to think that this character's destiny was sealed long before the narrative began on that fateful Friday and wants to set our affective compass from the start so that every move made, every scene described in the fictional socio-cultural and familial context in which Ana has presence, every chance occurrence, somehow inexorably contributes to a death foretold. The novel leaves a bitter taste, an uncomfortable ending; its affective force makes us wonder about the conditions that produce such a dramatic response to life by some women.

In the first chapter after the scene of the suicide, 'Ana sueña' (Ana Dreams), we join Ana early in the morning dropping of the kids at the bus stop and contemplating the same daily routine of catching a bus to work on smoggy streets, travelling with the same sad-faced people and afraid of catching a glimpse of herself in the bus's rear view mirror and discovering the same sad look on her own face. She decides that when she gets home she will call her boss, Mr Abe, and lie once again that the kids are sick and how she needs to stay home with them. She passes by the bakery and the smell of freshly baked rolls awakens memories of how her grandmother baked fresh rolls for her father in the afternoons, rolls that Ana was never allowed to taste. We get a quick sketch of a spoilt son, Ana's father, and a 'good mother', Libertad:

> They were just for Don Santiago, her father, who ate them with hot chocolate after dinner. I imagined them so soft and was dying to try them, fresh out of the oven, with the butter melting on a bit of sugar. Grandmother Libertad said that good mothers cook for their children, know their tastes and please them, but she would never let Gregoria [Ana's mother] in the kitchen to prepare dishes for her daughters. (Phé-Funchal 2015a: 22)

Crossing the street Ana is distracted by the church bells marking the hour, but 'that day she did not run, she didn't think about how little time she had to serve the dog his food, put on her high heels, do her make-up' (22). Since she is not going to work, she decides to take the route home past the apartment block where her and her husband Carlos had their first idyllic moments together. She sees their third-story apartment with the original white venetian blinds on the windows and imagines behind them her easel 'exploding with colours and with the symphony music that Carlos liked so much ringing in the background' (23). The same name is still on the apartment block, El Cielito, the name that she wanted to believe 'presaged eternal happiness' (23). She reflects on Carlos, who had died four years before, and remembers refusing to attend his funeral because of her dislike of funeral casks after her father's death: 'feeling like an intruder in a funeral in which the dead person did not belong to her, never occurred to her, she had as much right as that little bitch that accidentally forgot to take her contraceptive pills. Carlos was hers, no one else's' (23). We are given no further information at this point, but we are prompted to imagine an affair, a pregnancy, a separation, and an ongoing love for her husband. Instead of going to Carlos' funeral, she drops her kids off with her sisters and takes two sleeping pills, a habit learned several years earlier from her own mother's addiction developed after the death of her sister, Ana's aunt. She falls asleep and dreams of childhood visits to a farm during end of year holidays, recalling fond moments spent with her father, Don Santiago, but then also 'the beating for the episode with the chicken' (25). (The chicken incident is left hanging, unexplained, until it is taken up again in a later chapter.) Ana's dream at this point turns nightmarish and grotesque as she is conscious of herself wandering outside on the farm at night, being drawn to a sobbing sound coming from a bulk covered in a blanket, hundreds of crying women dressed in black and milling around her, her father and siblings lying face up and dressed in white robes, and the smell and look of her grandmother's decomposing body because her father had insisted on her being on display for four and half days of mourning, 'to make sure that grandma Libertad did not wake up in the tomb' (26). The next day Ana collects the children at dawn. While walking home she thinks of passing by the El Cielito apartment again, but decides against it, fearing 'that gnawing in the stomach, or the sensation of fear and anxiety that she gets when she feels like looking up at it, and maybe, just maybe, meeting Carlos's eyes' (27). As she enters the house her little yellow dog greets her. She 'tells him her plans, takes two tiny pills and asks him to wake her at 7.30' (27).

The whole plot of *Ana sonríe* is thus laid out in microcosm in the first fifteen pages. The main characters have been introduced, the deaths registered, and some of the underlying tensions in the lives of the main protagonist and her family have been revealed through sometimes bitter, sometimes nostalgic recollections. The rest of the novel will henceforth showcase each sister's affects and perceptions as they react to their daily routines and recall their own mixed experiences.

In the next chapter focused on Ana, 'Ana cuelga' (Ana Hangs Up), Ana chats briefly with her sister who reminds her to not miss any more days at work 'and end up like us' (41), though we are not told what this means. We assume it means loss of work and thus loss of income. One of the great fears of the middle class is to slide into poverty. This is reinforced as Ana recalls her childhood and the threat of parental sanction that always hung over her head. She recalls her mother Gregoria furiously erasing over and over again her old homework in her note book so that it could be written over again until the repeated rubbing left the pages wafer thin — the family budget was tight; things had to be recycled. At the same time her childhood memories are interlaced with images of her over-bearing father, Don Santiago, his obsession with his mother Libertad's death and his daily visits to the cemetery:

> He took charge of the cleaning and organising of the mausoleum, in which new flowers were placed every day — white, always white and fresh, as if the internment had just occurred. Her father believed that if the spirit of Libertad found the tomb adorned and him in front of it, she would see how much he missed her and perhaps would come out and talk with him. Thus a good part of the family budget, which Gregoria stretched as much as possible, ebbed away because Don Santiago, who never lacked work, believed that is was not dignified for a gentleman to pursue debts. (42)

Don Santiago, in Freudian fashion, idolizes his mother while occasionally verbally and physically abusing his wife and children. He fits the profile of the male who has rigid expectations of his family's members, displays little or no empathy for others' frailties and is usually characterized by angry outbursts and power-assertive behaviour—someone who rules and ridicules. The emotional and social impact of authoritarian parenting rebounds down the line in a causal chain: the narrator recalls the shame Ana felt after being chided by her teacher and teased by the other children when her fragile notebook pages tore: 'Girls and boys stood around her shouting you don't have a book, you're a great big sook, others called her poor and ugly, poor and ugly, poor and ugly' (43). Ana manages to escape when the children turn on Loretta and taunt her about her father being crazy and being seen standing for hours talking to a tomb. Ana hides in a shed, but becomes terrified and can't move when she sees a big spider eating a praying mantis. She remains in the shed until school is out and can't be found. Loretta goes home and tells their mother, Gregoria, who hurries to school to look for her. Eventually she is found by the school security guard, unable to talk and in a fever. Gregoria rushes home with her, because 'she's afraid of Don Santiago arriving and finding the little ones alone, getting angry with her, with Ana, with everyone and once again smashing dishes. But it's too late. The man is waiting at the entrance to the house, furious, his eyes injected with rage and with a closed fist' (44). He grabs Ana and roughly puts her in a cold bath to bring down the fever. She is put to bed and sleeps for two days. Her father visits her room and comforts her and laughs upon hearing the story of the spider. We get a profile of a father capable of violent rage, but also feelings deep affection for his family, an emotional Jekyll and Hyde. In the novel, anticipating the father's anger becomes a way of coping, but it creates fear and an authoritarian family structure. This is classic psychological and emotional behaviour of children traumatized by witnessing intra-familiar violence. Both males and females are affected, though differentially. Those who come from abusive homes often view violence as normal and carry it into their own relationships as adults — monkey see, monkey do.

This complexity and ambivalence remains with Ana her whole life. We learn that due to the shortage of money, she and her sisters become experts in recycling note books and decorating them. The practice becomes another subtle measure of their bonding. But notebooks play a further role in Ana's life: years later Ana would write down in her notebooks ways of communicating with her dead husband, who 'would hide and enjoy seeing her anxiety rise and make her cry' (48). She forgets to ring her boss, Mr Abe, until her phone rings and he's on the line asking her to come by the office early on Monday: 'Ana trembles. On the other end of the line Mr Abe spoke in the same tone as Carlos the time he said let's talk Monday, Ana' (48).

In another scene, 'Ana observa', another affective set piece, Ana is walking the dog when she happens to catch a glimpse of a woman through the window of a house. The woman is dusting the furniture. The scene has no causal link to anything, but like many of the chance events in the novel, it triggers key memories.

The woman doesn't notice Ana watching:

> She's concentrating, focused on calculating the exact time
> needed to finish polishing the book shelf and place the little
> statues, the photo, the porcelain in the precise spot, in the place
> that he likes, because the light hits it here and there, because from
> this angle — and in no other — you notice this detail of the photo
> from the gentleman's reading chair. The woman finishes placing
> everything in its place, takes a few steps back and contemplates
> — Ana assumes she is smiling — a master work of order. (102)

The narrator focalizes through the consciousness of both the
woman and the absent man ('in this angle — and in no other —
you notice this detail of the photo'). The woman's reverie in
placing valuable objects in exact order dictated by the man is
broken by an unexpected shout, the sound of something
breaking, a bus passing and suddenly 'the woman is holding a
toddler in her arms and telling off a dark-skinned girl in a plain
blouse to whom she hands the little boy dressed in blue' (102).
Why these details? This scene prompts Ana to freely associate
about her own children, about her sisters and her mother's
support in minding her kids, about the news of Lucretia's
hysterectomy, about her job in Mrs Abe's textile factory, the
excitement of getting to display her creative artistic abilities, the
death of Mrs Abe and the subsequent disappointment when
forced by Mr Abe to churn out commercial popular designs for
the local market instead of overseas customers. Ana recalls her
anger upon hearing Mr Abe's words: 'Ana, I need designs for
mothers, nothing elaborate or fine, something infantile. Mr Abe's
words resound once more and the rage begins to rise up through
Ana's body' (104). What we have is a set of micro-narrative events
re-assembled through free association, existing as little crypts on
Ana's mind and which all have a link in a chain of affect
contributing to her downfall. As the chapter closes, the omniscient narrator takes full control of focalization again as Ana's
dog senses her distress, pulls at his lead and brings her back to
the present, leading her away down the streets to the church
'where Ana had her first communion and where two days later
Lucretia had decided a mass would be performed over her body'
(104). We can now look back at the scene of the woman dusting,
her task not only to clean but to put things in order for a man who

has leisure time to read and contemplate favourite objects, which contrasts with Ana's recollection of her artistic hopes dashed by another man, Mr Abe. Likewise, the chance arrival of a bus signals danger as the females who do the child minding are reminded of their duty of care. This is Phé-Funchal's subtle way of referencing gender hierarchy and its division of labour without sermonising — a preachy narrator drawing conclusions for the reader. This is a carefully crafted novel.

Two chance events drive Ana's suicide: the crowded, dirty city streets with poor drainage produce a passing car which sprays filthy water on an unsuspecting pedestrian dressed to go to the opening of an exhibition, a fumbled apology from the driver, an offer to drive her home to change and accompany her to the same exhibition, the exchange of phone numbers, the subsequent courtship and cohabitation: thus Ana meets Carlos, a painter like her. The second chance event is linked to Carlos's secret lover apparently forgetting to take her contraceptive pill (referenced above), which sets in motion a causal chain as Carlos, out of misguided loyalty and a sense of obligation to social rules, decides he has to marry her. He never wanted children, he had told Ana. Ana had invested in her Blue Prince and was betrayed. Her inability to emotionally process the destruction of her relationship with Carlos leads her story to the suicidal denouement. Yet Ana's suicide could also be said to be made from a thousand cuts, the accumulated small moments of disappointment, derision and defraud she suffered through being bullied at school, through fear of her father's rage, through watching her mother and sisters being beaten, her authoritarian paternal grandmother's iron rule, her husband's philandering and his assuming authorship of her paintings, her disappointing suitors in New York, her sleazy boss in the textile factory, her career blocked, and so forth.

How to read these affective moments induced by chance events, triggered by smells and sounds and sudden sightings? We might begin to understand them by taking a short detour via Jacques Rancière's challenge to a certain way Gerard Genette reads Flaubertian description. According to Rancière, Genette implies that Flaubert's literary consciousness did not really understand what it was doing and that the affective moments of reverie, when his narrative 'freezes up' (the expression is Genette's), were dissociated from the narrative flow, 'moments of silence that interrupt the classical narrative logic of the action with its characters, events, and feelings' (Genette quoted in Rancière 2011: 121). Flaubert's literary consciousness 'was not and could not be at the level of his work and experience' (Ibid.). Rancière disagrees and reads the example of Charles and Emma's courting in *Emma Bovary* as not a freezing up or a de-acceleration in the action, but precisely the opposite:

> [T]his opposition between a straightforward logic of actions and moments of interruption does not hold. These moments—these fleeting compositions of autonomized affections and perceptions—in fact constitute the very texture of the characters' 'feelings' and of the 'events' that happen to them. Thus it is not a dreamlike suspension but a decisive acceleration of the action that is produced by the zones of 'silence' that, in Madame Bovary, compose the meeting between Charles and Emma. (Rancière 2011: 121)

Rancière appears to be saying that there is a time of affect which does not necessarily run at the pace of the main narrative flow, but which nevertheless drives the narrative forward — affective descriptions as a dimension of time itself, not mere adornments to the flow of narrative action but integral to that flow, even if such affect exists as a virtuality that we can only register through its traces. *Ana sonríe* is mostly composed of these traces of affect in objects and physical movement, such as the masterful evocation of solitude mixed with nostalgia, regret and anxiety in the opening of the very next chapter after Ana's walk with the dog ('Ana observa'). In 'Loretta llora' (Loretta Cries), male privilege and patriarchy are more directly on display. The third-person narrative focalizes through Loretta. She sits down to write, her father's fountain pen in hand and a blank white sheet of paper in front of her. But the words will not come. The green mug resting on the bureau brings to mind the past and the sisters' mother, Gregoria, and transforms the sounds of the end of the working day as they are absorbed by Loretta's body and drift up in synaesthesia through the steps, impregnating the walls of her office building:

> It is not every day that Loretta uses Gregoria's green cup. She only resorts to it when she needs to feel her mother close, when

she misses the silence that accompanied them for years of being mother and daughter living as if nothing else existed, as if the prolonged silences of Ana and Lucretia, occupied with their own lives, were an everyday thing from the beginning. Loretta listens to the footsteps of her co-workers and feels the familiar weekend nervousness climbing the steps, seeping through the walls and ringing next to the windows. She listens to them rinse their cups, close the drawers, remove the last papers from the machines, seal the envelopes that will be sent on Monday morning, and hears them say goodbye, see you Monday, see you later, have a great weekend, as the door is closed again and again and the footsteps fade on the stone path leading from the wooden building to the main street. (Phé-Funchal 2015a: 105)

There is an unmistakeable mood or *Stimmung*, which Phé Funchal does well to not specifically articulate in language. The cup is metonymically enchained with a blank sheet of white paper and a fountain pen as carriers and prompts for an indeterminate affect, whose intensification evokes a blockage, past experiences of loss, regret and disappointment in a complex structure of feeling, which neither Loretta nor the narrator can fully bring to consciousness but which the reader herself is left to contemplate and 'feel'. The key phrase is 'feels the familiar weekend nervousness.' What is meant here? Weekends of loneliness with no family of her own? We get a clue as the chapter progresses. Loretta imagines her mother's knotty hands and her fingernails caressing the green mug as she recalls the time Gregoria told her of her regrets for marrying Don Santiago:

while she tells her how she had left everything for Don Santiago and saying, as if to justify herself, that the only good thing to come of it, the only good thing for her, were them, her three daughters, and that she had always asked herself —and at this point she seemed to excuse herself even more — that if she had her time again, if she knew what awaited her, whether she would walk the same path again. (106)

Gregoria has internalised guilt, another legacy of self-abnegation for a man. This is the chapter in which the bitterness of Loretta's break-up with Edgar is revisited. The narration pulls back to reflect on how Gregoria 'had confessed this to her because Loretta wouldn't stop crying about Edgar' (106), to then focus in again on Loretta who remembers the futility of saving her virginity for years just for Edgar, who would eventually take up with another woman after getting her pregnant. The narration leaps further back in time still to relate how Gregoria, who inherited her mother's looks, was shielded from suitors by her hyper-protective brother, Rodolfo, who 'could not stand the idea of seeing her, the image of his mother, married to a man, even less, pregnant' (107). This kind of Freudian attachment is repeated in different form when the narrative switches back to Ana and an unflattering portrait emerges of the paternal grandmother, Libertad, her authoritarian rule and her obsessive concern for her son's welfare. Ana remembers frequently accompanying her grandmother to the municipal laundries to hire someone to wash fine quality clothes, but rarely finding anyone with whom she could be satisfied. Libertad is a tyrant. Upon seeing her, the washer women 'remember the beatings, the shouting, losing the work, and they trembled' (118). Libertad eventually finds a reliable washer woman, Coralia, who subsequently becomes attached to the family for years and who dotes on Ana. The moment is an occasion to remember Coralia's story, of how her mother was an illiterate country woman made pregnant by the farm owner, who had also fathered other illegitimate children.

Nevertheless, Coralia's mother is said to have loved her unconditionally. The stories she told resonated with Ana, who remembers asking her to always repeat the story of her cousin, Maura, who had married 'a proud man' without thinking it through, a man 'who treated her badly and let her see him going around with other women before finally packing her bags and dragging her back to her mother saying she was a bad woman' (120). But Maura remained in love with him and only after hearing that he had taken another woman and left the area for good, she went down to the river and drowned herself. Ana remembers with fondness Coralia's inner strength and confidence, of how she found a husband, an itinerant shoe repairer, whom she obliged to drop his prices in the neighbourhood for five months as proof of his devotion before agreeing to go out with him and marry him two months later. The last time Ana saw Coralia she was happy. She missed her deeply, missed 'feeling in her embrace a calm she would never feel again' (121).

Sometimes the portrayal of the sisters' memories is over-cooked and a bit artificial as their indulgence in fantasies of Hollywood-style romance are often a bit too naïve to believe for women from a middle-class background in our contemporary epoch (the novel does not give overt clues to the era, but references to paying for things with cards places it in recent history). While descriptive emotional excess is a constitutive ingredient in the affective fabric of melodrama, indeed expected, Phé-Funchal mostly keeps it under control. At other times, this ingenuousness is cancelled by the sister's striking back. We had left Loretta remembering her devastation at being jilted by Edgar, a trainee doctor who had told her he didn't want children, yet had gotten his girlfriend pregnant. Lucretia had already heard rumours of his cheating around town, but hadn't told Loretta. Loretta and Lucretia decide to gate-crash his informal birthday celebration at the house of his mother, Doña Nesle. The sisters arrive with a cake and are immediately and maliciously informed by Edgar's surprised mother that they were not expected for Edgar's 'engagement party'. Hackles are raised. Loretta parries back:

> well, well, what a great surprise, finally the doctor will fulfil his dreams. How strange that you haven't married before the pregnancy was so advanced. I congratulate you Doña Nesle, your daughter-in-law looks real fine, so good that we hope Edgar doesn't repeat his father's steps, right, because Edgar always says, right Eddie, how hard it was for you not to have your parents at your graduation like all the other students of the college. You're a good man. (182)

Acute embarrassment is felt by Edgar, his fiancée and Edgar's mother. But we are not done yet. Revenge is best served slowly. The cake is cut through clenched teeth and Loretta chooses the occasion to skewer the recently engaged couple. The narration drifts in and out of free indirect discourse and changing focalization, as Loretta boils inside, exposing and mocking Edgar's deceit:

> what is your future wife called, little Eddy, you've got a face of . . . I don't know, I can't put a name to you, it's difficult, as I don't know people like you, I'm not able to name you. You, you've got the face of a Marta, Loretta said, in that moment remembering

the sun glasses, women's ones, that she found months ago in the glove box of Edgar's car. They belong to Sister Marta, a little nun that left them in the bus during the last daytrip to a rural community, I put them away so no one would rob them, but I haven't had time to pass by the convent. (183)

The baiting is continued for a while until the sisters decide to leave. But the revenge is short-lived and of little consolation as Loretta cannot overcome her feelings for Edgar and breaks down crying in the car.

I have laboured the detail in many of the scenes described above because what Phé-Funchal does is create intense affect through memory, and these memories carry the more long-term plot line — the history of the family pieced together from fragments, especially traumatic moments. The actual events in the twelve-hour day are at best co-relevant information, merely marking clock time, but not the time of memory and affect, the three decades of key events which have shaped the psychological and emotional disposition of the sisters. The style is reminiscent of Virginia Woolf.[42] How should we judge such novels? One approach would be to indict the text for its lack of joy, its failure to offer happier, positive social role models for women. But in no way does it automatically follow that dominant fictional constructions of unhappy or troubled lives therefore imply that in Central America the practice of joy does not happen, that bodies don't act, that death is chosen over life. The reader draws her own conclusions, but not on the basis of a supposed lack of a redeeming character that might carry an uplifting message. Besides, Ana is a wonderfully crafted character who takes control of her life, even if that control leads to suicide. Her story shows how negative early experiences can have lasting emotional and psychological consequences due to male irresponsibility and authoritarian household rule. We are far from a nurturing and stable home life providing an emotionally stable environment for a child's development. The portraits of the three sisters are surely ones that women (and men) can relate to — character traits and life choices they see in other people's lives or even their own. What they demonstrate, regardless of the tragic ending, is intra-familiar gender solidarity in a man's world. In spite of the negative portrait of the paternal grandmother, Libertad, what stands out strongly are the friendships between the women: the sisters, their mother

Gregoria, aunt Carlotta, the washer woman, Coralia, memorably painted in brief brush strokes, and Mrs Arkes in New York, where Ana lived for eight years as she tried to make it as a painter. The moments when they are present produce acts of kindness and camaraderie. The one underdeveloped character is Gregoria, the sisters' mother. She deserves as much character construction as the silky tyranny of the paternal grandmother, Libertad, but perhaps this lack of full character development is meant to be symbolic of her abnegation and vice versa.

The antagonism which drives Phé-Funchal's novel and her short stories is the difference between the idealised world of 'good behaviours' and traditional gender roles (abnegation, rectitude, family honour, duty), to which women are historically shackled, versus the reality of their daily domestic life, with the ever-present threat of physical and verbal violence, the bitter fruit of over-bearing male authoritarianism and control of money. Phé-Funchal sketches a social reality in which women are inculcated, 'educated' into gender hierarchy and duty. This oscillation between appearance and reality provides the underlying binary semiotic system. But the issue of parental violence and control is not restricted to men, though they carry the main burden of blame. Women too are indicted, if not as harshly and only implicitly, for conforming to male control and dominance and thus perpetuating the cycle. For example, the cruelty of Don Santiago is confirmed in a later recollection of him and Libertad not allowing Gregoria to call a doctor at night for her six-month old baby that was in a fever. The baby dies. The image that is formed of Don Santiago is that of a man whose defects are largely the fault of his mother, Libertad.

If there is a fault in the book it is the universally depressing image of men, pretty much the same as in Escudos's narrative. Phé-Funchal paints a horror house of masculinity. But this need not be read off the surface of the text as a generalised condition of all male subjectivity in Central America, but merely the kinds of males who have all had an influence on the fictional female character's emotions and life choices, which helps the reader better understand how some women walk the path they do. Phé-Funchal is in no mood to provide redemptive male models here as she highlights the daily life of women in a context of male privilege and hostility, trying to balance domestic commitment with careers in the daily negotiation of sociality and care, the glue that keeps society in a state somewhat proximate to bearable, a high-wire act often overlooked by men in their relentless self-possession.

How much attention does Phé-Funchal really want us to pay to the suicide, then? In a way the novel calls forth the suicide as the need for some sort of ending. To leave the story dangling, inconclusive, would give no rhyme or reason for this particular slice of Ana's life compared to any other. In a kind of strange paradox, the suicide is the only movement forward in the narrative, since the rest of the book is basically a static present (the twelve hours of the novel's day) filled with affect-laden memories of disenchantment caused by males, punctuated by occasional small triumphs. It is telling that in the final scene of the novel, in order to hang herself, Ana makes a slip knot in a rope, something her father had taught her on the farm during Christmas holidays all those years ago. Ana's ultimate painting was her own life. It just wasn't what she had in mind when she started out, but at least she was in charge of the last brush stroke. The control of a woman over her own life also includes the right to end it.

Notes

1 Barthes 1975: 24–5.
2 Examples would be literature written by figures such Sergio Ramírez, Ana María Rodas and Ana Cristina Rossi, to name just a few. While their work was read, it did not hold the same attention as testimonial literature, itself bolstered and championed by the US academy. For critiques of testimonial literature vis-à-vis the US academy, see: Gugelberger 1996.
3 Julie Marchio sees the genealogy running from at least Rosario Aguilar's 1965 *Quince barrotes de izquierda a derecha* and Claribel Alegría's *Cenizas de Izalco* (1966), through Anacristina Rossi's *María la noche* (1985) and *Limón reggae* (2007), *El Corazón del silencio* (2004) by Tatiana Lobo, Carol Zardetto's *Con Pasión Absoluta* (2005), and Vanessa Núñez Handal's *Los locos mueren de viejos* (2008), to name the most prominent. (Marchio 2017, in press – Marchio has kindly allowed her essay to be quoted)
4 Vania Vargas, Tania Hernández, Salvador Canjura, Rodrigo Soto, Javier Payeras, Maurice Echeverría, Warren Ulloa, Catalina Murillo, Byron Quiñónez, Javier Mosquera, Marilinda Guerrero, Álvaro Rojas Salazar, María del Carmen Pérez Cuadra, etc. The lists here and above are a minimum representation of contemporary Central American writers and run the inevitable risk of being taken as a description of the contemporary canon. Nothing could be further from my intentions, though canons are inevitable, no matter what we think of them, simply because some writers are judged by the critics to be better, more original or more interesting than others and/or have more of their works sold in wider distribution networks. For the problems of canon formation and literary markets, see Dante Liano (2012).
5 Werner Mackenbach refers to how Central America from the 1980s and 1990s onwards 'experiences a real *boom* in its narrative literature, especially as regards the number of publications and the diversity of literary production' (Mackenbach 2007: n/p.).
6 Foucault 1997: 323.
7 Heine quoted in Lukács 1981: 61.
8 This double marginalization has occurred throughout Central

161

America. For example, in the cases of Costa Rica and Nicaragua with respect to Afro-descendant and Indigenous peoples: in the case of Costa Rica, the black world on the Caribbean coast, and in the case of Nicaragua, much more so in terms of the ethnic diversity with Afro-Nicaraguan and Indigenous populations. For Costa Rica, see Quince Duncan (1975), the first Costa Rican Afro-Caribbean writer to write in Spanish; and in the case of Nicaragua, Lizandro Chávez Alfaro (1999). In addition, there are numerous women writers, especially poets, of Afro descent. For a judicious treatment of Afro-descendant Caribbean writers of Central America, see Mosby 2012.

9 Zee Edgell, Glen Godfrey, Felicia Hernandez, George Seymour Gabb, James Sullivan Martinez, John Alexander Watler, Leo Bradley, Milton Arana, Nicholas Anthony Ignatius Pollard, Raymond Barrow, Zelma Edgell and Zoila Ellis-Browne are the most prominent. One struggles to find mention anywhere of novels and short stories in Spanish.

10 An old man on his death who recalls the foundations of a small rural town isolated from national affairs, but which nevertheless suffers their pathologies; a patriarchal figure tied to a tree and left in the elements; houses painted political colours; mysterious strangers who arrive and disturb the town's harmony, etc., are all nods to García Márquez's magnum opus. Similarly, the rural speech patterns and customs of Rulfo's novel find echo in Río Viejo and the narration even mimic's the opening of Juan Rulfo's *Pedro Páramo*: the village 'sits on the coals of the earth, at the *very mouth of hell*' ('the village was at the very mouth of Purgatory' in *Got seif*). *Got seif de Cuin!* is rooted in regional particularities, much the same as Rulfo and García Márquez (and one of his major influences, Faulkner). *Got seif de Cuin!* is suffused with orality and popular culture as resources to recreate the environment from the point of view of the people, especially their bewilderment at the impact of national political events on their settled life: the changing of the guard as Spain, Fayabón (Guatemala) and England try to impose their expansionist territorial drives onto the region and its administrative power structure, which dominates the townspeople's lives. There are other similarities with Macondo: a people that suffers the pathologies of modernity, but not the benefits and that lives a series of political agitations that the inhabitants do not understand very well. There is an old man, Don Enrique, who functions as the main focal point for linking episodes, such as Aureliano Buendía in *One Hundred Years*. The story is told from the limited perspective of the people who have to get accustomed to the strangers who one day arrive and who change the traditional life and involve the people in national

affairs. As in *One Hundred Years*, the trajectory of the town is narrated with abundant humour and irony, perhaps the best way to approach national history, but with a much lighter touch: the action in *Got seif de Cuin!* does not occur within an encompassing tragic framework which projects a pessimistic vision of history, a fact that distances Ruiz Puga's novel from *One Hundred Years* and the novels of the Boom in general. Boom novels reacted against the socialist-realist and naturalist novels that came before them in terms of form — modernist technique replaces realism — but there is no profound revolution in content, even when the scenario shifts to urban spaces. The Boom novels imitated their naturalist predecessors in terms of their biologism and racial determinism and, crucially, their pessimistic appraisal of the capacity of the popular classes to enter modernity. This is why the Boom narratives exhibit tragic and existentialist portrayals of Latin American reality. Not so Ruiz Puga. Whether this is so because of Belize's largely non-militaristic independence movement or Ruiz Puga's Christian faith, we are far from a tragic vision.

11   'I am at the barber's, and a copy of *Paris-Match* is offered to me. On the cover, a young Negro in a French uniform is saluting, with his eyes uplifted, probably fixed on a fold of the tricolour. All this is the meaning of the picture. But whether naively or not, I see very well what it signifies to me: that France is a great Empire, that all her sons, without any colour discrimination, faithfully serve under the flag, and that there is no better answer to the detractors of an alleged colonialism than the zeal shown by this Negro in serving his so-called oppressors' (Barthes 1972:115).

12   I attempted to capture this settling of accounts and other cultural criticism by Ramírez in Browitt 2004.

13   The real historical events are there, but re-fashioned through literary invention. Here reception is supremely important, since without it the novel does not exist. But reception is hardly controllable or even predictable and *Margarita* can be read in different ways: as a 'faithful' slice of Nicaraguan national history (a politically progressive, Leftist reception), or as one writer's aesthetic re-enactment of national history through personal perspective and memory, the focus on art rather than fact. It is a question of which reader the author had in mind, either or both.

14   Blandón 2010:104–26.

15   The life of Carmen Aguirre, La Caimana, is told in Victoria González-Rivera's 'The Alligator Woman's Tale' 2014.

16   Ramírez , quoted in Mackenbach 2000.

17   The Contras (literally, those against) were the US-backed paramilitaries fighting against the revolutionary Sandinista government.

18 For Lacan, the Real is the traumatic kernel, masked by the social structure and sitting behind it, which nevertheless affects subjectivity and its functioning The Real is not 'reality', but everything that lies outside and within the subject, but is not directly accessible. For Slavoj Žižek, assiduous follower and interpreter of Lacan, symbolization, or representation, will never comprehend reality sufficiently, which can never be fully revealed 'in itself'. The aspects of reality that resist being symbolized assume the form of a spectre, that is, an unsettling (ideological) closure (Žižek 1994: 21).

19 It is interesting to note that around this time such characters begin to appear with frequency in Central American novels, as in Rodrigo Rey Rosa's *El cojo bueno* (1996) and Horacio Castellanos Moya's *El arma en el hombre* (2001). The aesthetic 'recycling' of these personages mirrors the real-life recycling of demobilized combatants. *Sopa de caracol* (2002) by Arturo Arias, *Limón reggae* (2008) by Anacristina Rossi and *Camino de hormigas* (2014) by Miguel Huezo Mixco continue the sub-genre. Though these novels have their undoubted merits, are heterogeneous and do not present one-dimensional and stereotypical images of ex -fighters, they run the risk of becoming a species of *nuevo costumbrismo*.

20 S. Žižek, *God in Pain*, Kindle Location 734–5.

21 See 'Otro zoo' and 'El hijo de Ash'. Also see 'La niña que nunca tuve' (The Daughter I Never Had), from *Ningún lugar sagrado* (1998).

22 https://commons.wikimedia.org/wiki/File:Rembrandt_ Abraham_en_Isaac,_1634.jpg

23 https://commons.wikimedia.org/wiki/File:The_Sacrifice_of_ Isaac_by_Caravaggio.jpg

24 René Girard 1972, *La Violence et le Sacré*, Paris: Grasset; Carol Delaney 1998: *Abraham on Trial*, Princeton University Press; Georges 1992: *Theory of Religion*, Zone Books.

25 A similar staging of ethical decision-making in the face of both ecological crisis and violence can be found in recent Hollywood blockbuster movies like *Noah* (2014) and *The Dawn of the Planet of the Apes* (2014, a creative re-make of the iconic *Planet of the Apes*, 1968). Though both films ply a middle ground of normative affect (with frequent sentimentality and didacticism), they also stage scenes of ecological crisis, as do many recent Hollywood disaster movies. But in *Noah* there is a dual philosophical drama: the question of the preservation of human life as well as the vitality of ecological systems. The film begins with a devastated environmental landscape. Noah has interpreted a sign of God, Yahweh, who urges him to build an ark and rescue all non-human species before the flood that will destroy all fallen human beings. Noah concludes that he and his family must also die so that the whole human race is

destroyed. Nevertheless, he is willing to allow his family to live as eventually they will all die of natural causes. However, in the ark a baby is born to the eldest son and his partner, a female rescued from the civil strife raging outside. The baby can reproduce and perpetuate the human race, so Noah decides to kill her. He raises the knife, but cannot go through with what he otherwise interprets as divine will. Compassion for an innocent human being prevents him from killing in the name of what he believes is divine revelation. Noah shows mercy and receives grace in the fictional construct – not from God, but from the audience as we are ethically and affectively positioned by the filmic narrative. Of course this moment in the film does not exist in the story of Noah in the Old Testament, but it is the right of art, of the aesthetic act, to place it there with philosophical-ethical intent. Contra the biblical parable of Abraham, in *Noah* no messenger of God intervenes. Noah is the one who must decide. As with 'Gracia', intuitive ethics triumph over the Law. Faith has the power to suspend the ethical in individuals, but it is a power we must resist.

26 It is important to note that perhaps the first to write about growing up Jewish in Guatemala was Víctor Perera, 1992: *Rites: A Jewish Childhood in Guatemala*.

27 'The day after turning ten, I was split in two. It was August 1981. Guatemala was a mess. I remember shootings, stray bullets, fights in the streets and ravines and even one in front of my school, with all the students being held inside. I remember the new security guard coming into the house at night and sitting next to the front door wrapped in a poncho, a huge shotgun in his lap and a warm thermos of coffee in his hands. I remember the sound of my father's words – not so much the words as the sound they made – when he announced that we would leave the country.'

28 Alexandra Ortiz regards this as indicative of how in post-war Central American literature, 'the violence is contained indirectly, submerged and allegorical, which makes the narration transform into one which direct social denunciation no longer appears' (Ortiz Wallner : 'Una escritura', 34).

29 For Raymond Williams, the term is preferred 'to emphasize a distinction from more formal concepts of "world-view' or "ideology" . . . .We are concerned with meanings and values as they are actively lived and felt, and the relations between these and formal or systematic beliefs are in practice variable . . . An alternative definition would be structures of experience . . . We are talking about characteristic elements of impulse, restraint, and tone; specifically affective elements of consciousness and relationships' (Williams 1977: 132).

30 Quoted in Lenson 1989: 573.

31 If there is one story with a flaw in it, it is this one. In a narrative aside, we are told rather didactically about the intensification of the war between the army and the guerrillas: 'I lived everything as an over-protected child lives everything: with innocence and candour and as if the different manifestations of violence were also part of a game. My father's recently contracted bodyguard (Mario) and was a defender in football games in the afternoon; the nightly gun fights were Luke and Han Solo and the other Jedi defeating the Galactic Empire' (106). By this stage in the collection of stories we already know that the child is living a sheltered life largely quarantined from the larger socio-economic and political reality. We don't need to have this explained. This is a very rare weak moment in what is otherwise a beautifully crafted set of short stories.

32 It is interesting to note the counterpoint to the deconstruction of patriarchal authority in Rey Rosa's 'Gracia' and the young girl's agency. Here, the paternal figure is all important and orients the child's sense of security faced with the preciousness of life in a situation of civil war.

33 'Larga noche hacia mi madre recounts the history of a settling of accounts with myself. The relationship with my mother was a web of non-sayings, tacit agreements and contradictions. Telling the story of her last night in the world, which took decades to happen, I thought I could tell the story of our family and my own history and bring them together as one, with their atavistic baggage of curses, secrets, failures and tragedies that make up the common history of an incestuous, endogenous and suffocating society like ours' (Cortés 2017).)

34 This also concords with Silke-Maria Weineck's strong linking of *pater* and *patria* and her much more universal claim that theories of political power all over the Western world 'are inextricably interwoven with theories of fatherhood, and that thus each redefinition of legitimate political rule will have to address the role of paternal power— and vice versa' (Weineck 2014: 109).

35 It is significant that in Cortés's most recent 2015 novel, *Mojiganga* (recently re-published in 2017 with Editorial Costa Rica), the underlying problematic is masculinity and violence in the 1980s in Central America personified in the novel by fictional recreations of state actors like the ex-Dominican president-dictator, Rafael Trujillos, among others. A *mojiganga* is a large paper maché figure constructed for carnivals and festivals and worn by someone to parade down the street. It is no surprise that among other things, the novel is about masks and charades. Echoes of Weineck's *Gschnas* and the masks of masculinity abound: 'Like the Gschnas, the figure of the

father is cobbled together of bits and pieces, some useful, some obsolete, a bricolage of fear and desire, a repetition of memories and symptoms, of ancient mythologemes and fading ideologemes. The paternal system that had proven so resilient under millennia of repeated onslaughts enters a rapid oscillation: deeply entrenched in the collective psyche, and an object of derision and ridicule; part Darth Vader, part Homer Simpson' (Weineck 2014: 174–5).

36 One year after *El desencanto* Escudos published a collection of short stories under the title *Felicidad doméstica y otras cosas aterradoras* (2002), in which the deconstruction of the abnegated motherhood is taken much further. In El tenedor de mamá' (Mum's Fork), for example, a daughter approaches her mother as she is cooking in the kitchen, flipping over pieces of fried banana in hot oil with a fork. The daughter is met with shouts of abuse. She fires back: 'I began shouting insults, how she should respect me, that I wasn't a little animal from the street that she took in out of Christian charity, that I was her daughter and deserved better treatment. Then she turned around and stuck the fork in my right eye' (65).

37 For Yajaira Padilla: 'While Escudos's fiction participates in a larger discussion of neoliberalism and its negative effects, her portrayal of female agency, use of violence, and desire brings to the forefront issues of gender that are absent in other literary works of the postwar period. Escudos not only develops the cynical and dysfunctional relationship between Boris and Rossana as symptomatic of the violent and embittered period of transition that El Salvador is living, but also draws a parallel between the obstacles and limitations women in general face with those that the woman writer faces in a profession dominated by men. In doing so, this piece calls into question the type of national identity that will result if only male voices are heard and the stories women have to tell are silenced and sublimated' (Padilla 2008: 142–3.

38 When asked in an 2005 interview for *Istmo* journal about the function of the body in her narrative and the question of pleasure denied, Escudos replied: 'Pleasure is denied, of course, denied by the environment, norms, prejudices, religion, society, impositions, fears of the individual. Personally, it is difficult for me to conceive of pleasure disconnected from love. Unfortunately, love is one of those categories which people distrust and flee from as from the devil himself. People have a horror of loving, of surrendering, of opening up and trusting in another person. In part it is understandable because there are men and women alike who have used love as an instrument of domination, humiliation, pain. Society is losing the ability to love, and with it, the ability to feel pleasure, especially at a spiritual level. And the spirit lives in a container called body and

they cannot be disconnected from each other.' Werner Mackenbach & Alexandra Ortiz Wallner, 'Jacinta Escudos – La continuidad en la discontinuidad,' *Istmo* 10, Foro,

39 The episodic play explores issues of consensual and non-consensual sex.

40 Gayle Rubin summarizes what is at issue thus: 'There have been two strains of feminist thought on the subject. One tendency has criticized the restrictions on women's sexual behavior and denounced the high costs imposed on women for being sexually active. This tradition of feminist sexual thought has called for a sexual liberation that would work for women as well as for men. The second tendency has considered sexual liberalization to be inherently a mere extension of male privilege. This tradition resonates with conservative, anti-sexual discourse' (Rubin 1984: 301).

41 Besides Jacinta Escudos, Denise Phé-Funchal and Carlos Cortés, Julie Marchio identifies Rosario Aguilar, Anacristina Rossi, Vanessa Núñez Handal and Tatiana Lobo as writers deconstructing hegemonic, normative notions of motherhood. See Marchio 2017.

42 Jacques Rancière sees Woolf's narrative this way: 'This is what Virginia Woolf does by reducing the plot to a minimum, to the point that the succession of things as they happen, one after the other, is almost confounded with the simple proceedings of a day or of a life: family stories that last the length of a day, with its changing lights and its varied tasks, or the length of a life, with the activities and the dreams specific to each age, from children's games to death including the university years, occupations of adulthood, marriage and maternity' (Rancière 2016: 49).

References

Acevedo, R. L. 1982: *La novela centroamericana. Desde el Popol-Vuh hasta los umbrales de la novela actual.* Río Piedras: Editorial Universitaria.

Ahmed, S. 2010: Happy Objects. In M. Gregg and G. Seigworth (eds) *The Affect Theory Reader.* Durham: Duke University Press.

Arias, A. 2007: *Taking Their Word. Literature and the Signs of Central America.* Minneapolis: University of Minnesota Press.

Aristophanes 1987: *The Birds.* Trans. A.H. Sommerstein, Warminster, Wiltshire (Eng.): Aris & Phillips.

Barthes, R. 1972: *Mythologies.* Trans. A. Lavers. London: Paladin.

—— 1975: *The Pleasure of the Text.* Trans. Richard Miller. New York: Hill and Wang.

Bataille, G. 1992: *Theory of Religion.* Zone Books.

Blandón, E. 2010: 'Rubén Darío: mutilación y monumentalización'. *Rubén Darío. Cosmopolita arraigado.* J. Browitt & W. Mackenbach (eds.). Managua: Instituto de Historia de Nicaragua y Centroamérica, 104–126.

Breaking the Waves. 1996: Dir. L. von Trier. Zentropa Entertainments. DVD.

Browitt, J. 2002: *Exorcizando los fantasmas del pasado nacional: Got seif de Cuin!* de David Ruiz y *Margarita, está linda la mar.* In *Istmo* 3, http://istmo.denison.edu/n03/articulos/fantasmas.html

Browitt, J. 2004: Amor perdido: Sergio Ramírez, la ciudad letrada y las fallas en el sandinismo gramsciano. *Istmo* 8, http://istmo.denison.edu/n08/articulos/amor.html

Brunner, J. J. 1998: *Globalización cultural y posmodernidad.* Santiago de Chile: Fondo de Cultura Económica.

Canepari-Labib, M. 2005: Linguistic Hybridity and Fragmented Identities in Belizean Literature. In S. Albertazzi, C. Pelliconi and M. Bondi, Marina (eds) *Cross-Cultural Encounters: New Languages, New Sciences, New Literatures.* Rome: Edizioni Officina, 109–119.

Castellanos Moya, H. 1996: *El asco, Thomas Bernhard en San Salvador.* San Salvador: Arcoiris.

Chacón, A., Mackenbach, W. and Nitschack, H. (eds) 2016: El Caribe y Centroamérica — Intersecciones y sincretismos transculturales. In

References

Ístmica 19, https://rediscablog.wordpress.com/2017/03/09/revista-istmica-no-19-2016/

Chakrabarty, D. 2016: Whose Anthropocene? A Response. In R. Emmett and T. Lekan (eds) *Whose Anthropocene? Revisiting Dipesh Chakrabarty's 'Four Theses'*. RCC Perspectives.

Chang, K. 2008: Disrupting Boundaries of Desire: Gender, Sexuality, and Globalization in Tsai Ming-liang's cinema of the oppressed. Electronic Doctoral Dissertation. Hong Kong University Library.

Chávez Alfaro, L. 1999: *Columpio al aire*. Managua: UCA.

Coeckelbergh, M. and Gunkel, D. 2014: Facing animals: A relational, other-oriented approach to moral standing. In *Journal for Agricultural and Environmental Ethics* 27 (5): 715–733.

Cortés, C. 2017: Mi nombre es orfandad. *Revista penúltima*, http://revistapenultima.com/mi-nombre-es-orfandad-de-carlos-cortes/

Cortés, C. 2017: *Mojiganga*. San José: Editorial Costa Rica.

——— 2012: *Larga noche hacia mi madre*. Madrid: Alfaguara.

——— 2010: *La última aventura de Batman*. San José: Uruk.

——— 2007: *La gran novela perdida. Historia personal de la narrativa costarrisible*. San José: Editorial Perro Azul.

——— 2002: *Tanda de cuatro con Laura*. Madrid: Alfaguara.

——— 1999: *Cruz de olvido*. México, D.F.: Alfaguara.

——— 1986: *Encendiendo un cigarrillo con la punta de otro*. Heredia: Editorial de la Universidad Nacional.

Cortez, B. 2010: *La estética del cinismo*. Guatemala City: F&G Editores.

Craft, L. 2013: Viajes fantásticos: cuentos de [in]migración e imaginación de Claudia Hernández. In *Revista Iberoamericana* LXXIX (242): 181–94.

Delaney, C. 1998: *Abraham on Trial: The Social Legacy of Biblical Myth*. Princeton: Princeton University Press.

Derrida, J. 2009: *The Animal That Therefore I Am*. Fordham University Press, Kindle Edition.

Dröscher, B. 2004: Huérfanas y otras sin madre. In *Revista de Crítica Literaria Latinoamericana* 30 (59): pp. 267–295.

Duncan Moodie, Q. 1975: *El negro en la literatura costarricense*. San José: Editorial Costa Rica.

Dupuy, J-P. 2013: *La marque du sacré*. Paris: Flammarion.

Ensler, E. 1996: *The Vagina Monologues*. Virago Press.

Escudos, J. 2015: . Madrid: Alfaguara.

——— 2010: *Crónicas para sentimentales*. Guatemala City: F&G Editores

——— 2008: *El Diablo sabe mi nombre*. San José: Uruk Editores.

——— 2005: Flotante: David Ruiz Puga más allá del exotismo. *Istmo* 19, http://istmo.denison.edu/n10/foro/ruiz.html

——— 2003: *A-B-Sudario*. Madrid: Alfaguara.

170

References

—— 2002: *Felicidad doméstica y otras cosas aterradoras*. Editorial X.

—— 2001: *El desencanto*. San Salvador: Dirección de Publicaciones e Impresos.

—— 1997: *Cuentos sucios*. San Salvador: Dirección de Publicaciones e Impresos.

—— 1993: *Contra-corriente*. San Salvador: UCA Editores.

——1987: *Apuntes de una historia de amor que no fue*. San Salvador: UCA Editores.

Ette, O., Kraume, A. Mackenbach, W. and Müller, G. (eds) 2012: *El Caribe como paradigma. Convivencias y coincidencias históricas, culturales y estéticas*. Berlin: Edition tranvía, Verlag Walter Frey.

Ette, O., Mackenbach, W., Müller, G. and Ortiz Wallner, A. (eds.) 2011: *Trans(it)Areas. Convivencias en Centroamérica y el Caribe*. Berlin: Edition tranvía, Verlag Walter Frey.

Foucault, M. 1997: The masked philosopher. In P. Rabinow (ed.), *The essential works of Foucault 1954–1984, Vol I. Ethics: subjectivity and truth*. New York: The New Press, 321–8.

Freud, S. 1917: Mourning and Melancholia. In *The Standard Edition of the Complete Psychological Works of Sigmund Freud, Volume XIV (1914–1916): On the History of the Psycho-Analytic Movement, Papers on Metapsychology and Other Works*. London: Hogarth Press, 243–258.

Galich, F. 2017: *Perrozompopo y otros cuentos latinoamericanos*. Managua: Anamá ediciones.

—— 2012: *Tikal Futura. Memorias para un futuro incierto (novelita futurista)*. Guatemala: F&G Editores.

—— 2000: *Managua Salsa City. ¡Devórame otra vez!* Managua: Anamá Editores.

Girard, R. 1972 : *La Violence et le Sacré*. Paris: Grasset.

Gómez Menjívar, J. C. 2011. Liminal Citizenry: Black Experience in the Central American Intellectual Imagination. Electronic Thesis or Dissertation. Ohio State University.

Gómez Menjívar, J. C. 2016: Precious Water, Priceless Words: Fluidity and Mayan Experience on the Guatemalan-Belizean Border. *Diálogo* 19 (1): 23–32.

González, A. 2002: *La muerte de Acuario*. Managua: Distribuidora Cultural.

Gugelberger, G. M. (ed.) 1996: *The Real Thing: Testimonial Discourse and Latin America*, Durham: Duke University Press.

Halbertal, M. 2012: *On Sacrifice*. Princeton: Princeton University Press.

Halfon, E. 2015: *Signor Hoffman*. Barcelona: Libros del Asteroide.

—— 2012: *Monasterio*. Barcelona: Libros del Asteroide.

—— 2012: *Elocuencias de un tartamudo*. Valencia: Editorial Pre-Textos.

—— 2011: *Mañana nunca lo hablamos*. Valencia: Editorial Pre-Textos.

—— 2017: *Clases de chapín*. Logroño: Fulgencio Pimentel.

—— 2010: *Los espacios irónicos*. Montevideo: La Propia Cartonera.

—— 2010: *La pirueta*. Valencia: Editorial Pre-Textos.

—— 2009: *Clases de dibujo*. AMG.

—— 2008: *El boxeador polaco*. Valencia: Editorial Pre-Textos.

—— 2008: *Clases de hebreo*. AMG.

—— 2007: *Siete minutos de desasosiego*. Bogotá: Panamericana Editorial.

—— 2004: *El ángel literario*. Barcelona: Anagrama.

—— 2003: *Esto no es una pipa, Saturno*. Madrid: Alfaguara.

—— 2003: *De cabo roto*. Santa Fé: Littera.

Heidegger, M. 1977: *The Question Concerning Technology and Other Essays*. trans. W. Lovitt. New York & London: Garland.

Hernández, C. 2017: *Roza, tumba, quema*. Bogotá: Laguna libros.

—— 2013: *Causas Naturales*. Prisa Ediciones.

—— 2007: *De fronteras*. Guatemala City: Piedra Santa.

—— 2005: *Olvida Uno*. San Salvador: Índole Editores.

—— 2002: *Mediodía de frontera*. San Salvador: Dirección de Publicaciones e Impresos.

—— 2001: *Otras ciudades*. San Salvador: Alkimia.

Hernández, J. 2016: *Dígame quién soy yo, madre*. San José: Ediciones Diagonal.

Jameson. F. 2015: *The Antinomies of Realism*. London: Verso.

Jossa, E. 2014: Cuerpos y espacios en los cuentos de Claudia Hernández: Decepción y resistencia. In *Centroamericana* 24 (1): 5–37.

Kokotovic, Misha. 2014: Telling Evasions: Postwar El Salvador in the Short Fiction of Claudia Hernández. In *A Contracorriente* 11 (2): 53–75.

—— 2003: After the Revolution: Central American Literature in the Age of Neoliberalism. In *A Contracorriente* 1 (1): 19–50.

Lenson, D. 1989: Herodiade. *The Massachusetts Review* 30 (4): 573–88.

Liano, D. 2012: El canon literario hispanoamericano actual, in B. Cortez, A. Ortiz Wallner, and V. Ríos Quesada (eds.) *(Per)versiones de la modernidad: literaturas, identidades y desplazamientos*. Guatemala: F&G Editores, 141–62.

Lukács G. 1981: *The Historical Novel*, trans. H & S. Mitchell, Harmondsworth: Penguin.

Mackenbach, W. 2014: Tróp(ic)os en movimiento — retos transnacionales/transareales para los estudios de las literaturas caribeñas y centroamericanas. In *Cahiers d'études romanes* 28: 15–32.

Mackenbach, W. 2008: El Caribe y la literatura centroamericana: de la doble exclusión al doble espejo. In O. Ette (ed.) *Caribbean(s) on the Move — Archipiélagos literarios del Caribe*. Frankfurt am Main, Berlin, Bern, Bruxelles, New York, Oxford, Wien: Peter Lang, 107–119.

Mackenbach, W. 2007: Entre política, historia y ficción. Tendencias en la narrativa centroamericana a finales del siglo XX. *Istmo* 15,

References

http://collaborations.denison.edu/istmo/n15/articulos/mackenbach2.html

Mackenbach, W. 2001: Novela de posguerra: *Managua, Salsa City (¡Devórame otra vez!)*. *Ancora: Suplemento Cultural de La Nación*. San José, Costa Rica, Domingo 13 de mayo.

Mackenbach, W. 2000: La nueva novela histórica en Nicaragua y Centroamérica. In *Istmo* 2000, http://istmo.denison.edu/n01/articulos/novela.html

Mackenbach, W. and Ortiz Wallner, Alexandra. 2005: Jacinta Escudos — La continuidad en la discontinuidad. *Istmo* 10, Foro, http://istmo.denison.edu/n10/foro/escudos.html

Marchio, J. 2017 : Violence au féminin: Mères castratrices et filles assassins. In A. Reynes-Delobel and D. Barrientos Tecún (eds) *Femmes et littérature dans les Amériques, actes du colloque IDA 2013*. AMU: Aix-en-Provence (forthcoming).

Marion, J. L. 2011: Sketch of a Phenomenological Concept of Sacrifice. In J.L. Marion *The Reason of the Gift* (Richard Lectures). University of Virginia Press. Kindle Edition.

Noah 2014: Dir. D. Aronofsky, Paramount Pictures, DVD.

McGowan, T. 2017: The Bankruptcy of Historicism: Introducing Disruption into Literary Studies. In R. Sbriglia (ed.) *Everything You Always Wanted to Know about Literature but Were Afraid to Ask Žižek*. Durham: Duke University Press, 89–106.

Menton, S. 1993: *La nueva novela histórica de la América Latina*, Austin: University of Texas Press.

Mosby, D. E. 2012: 'Raíces y rutas: Identidad, ciudadanía, y la negritud transnacional en la literatura de afrodescendientes centroamericanos. In B. Cortez, A. Ortiz Wallner, and V. Ríos Quesada (eds.) *(Per)versiones de la modernidad: literaturas, identidades y desplazamientos*. Guatemala: F&G Editores, 317–343.

Ortiz Wallner, A. 2014: Una escritura más allá de las fronteras: la narrativa f(r)iccional de Eduardo Halfon. In *Hispanorama* 144: 34–38.

—— 2013: Claudia Hernández — por una poética de la prosa en tiempos violentos. In *LEJANA. Revista Crítica de Narrativa Breve* 6:1–10.

—— 2012: *El arte de ficcionar: la novela contemporánea en Centroamérica*. Madrid: Iberoamericana; Frankfurt: Vervuert.

Padilla, Y. M. 2008: Setting 'La diabla' Free: Women, Violence, and the Struggle for Representation in Postwar El Salvador. *Latin American Perspectives* 35(5), 133–45.

Perera, V. 1992: *Rites: A Jewish Childhood in Guatemala*. New York: Hippocrene Books.

Pérez, Y. 2014: Memory and Mourning in Contemporary Latin American Literature: A Reading of Claudia Hernández' *De fronteras*. *Habana elegante*,

http://www.habanaelegante.com/Spring_Summer_2014/
Invitation_Perez.html

—— 2013: Historias de metamorfosis: lo abyecto, los límites entre lo
animal y lo humano, en la literatura centroamericana de posguerra.
In *Revista Iberoamericana* LXXIX (242): 163–80.

Perkowska, M. 2011: La infamia de las historias y la ética de la escritura
en la novela centroamericana contemporánea. *Istmo* 24,
istmo.denison.edu/n22/articulos/24.html

Phé-Funchal, D. 2017: Cuenta Centroamérica, Portal literario.
http://www.goethe.de/ins/mx/lp/prj/lit/aut/gua/
es13159851.htm

——2015a: *Ana sonríe*. Guatemala City: F&G Editores.

—— 2015b: *La habitación de la memoria*. Madrid: Alfaguara.

—— 2015c: Conociendo a 'Ana sonríe' de Denise Phé-Funchal. In
Elsalvador.com: Entretenimiento, http://www.elsalvador.com/
entretenimiento/156516/conociendo-a-ana-sonrie-de-denise-
phe-funchal/

—— 2011: *Buenas Costumbres*. Guatemala City: F&G Editores.

—— 2010: *Manual del Mundo Paraíso*. Guatemala City: Catafixia
Editores.

—— 2007: *Las Flores*. Guatemala City: F&G Editores.

—— n/d. Denise Phé-Funchal. In Goethe Institut online. Cuenta
Centroamérica,
http://www.goethe.de/ins/mx/lp/prj/lit/aut/gua/
es13159851.htm

Piekarski, M. 2016: The Problem of the Question About Animal Ethics:
Discussion with Mark Coeckelbergh and David Gunkel. In *Journal
for Agricultural Environmental Ethics* 29: 705–715.

Quirós, D. 2014: Driving the City: Contesting Neoliberal space in
Managua, Salsa City. In *Romance Notes* 54 (1): 9–14.

Rancière, J. 2016: *The Lost Thread: The Democracy of Modern Fiction*. New
York: Bloomsbury Academic.

Rancière, J. 2011: *Mute Speech*. Trans. J. Swenson. New York: Columbia
University Press.

Rancière, J. 2006: *The Politics of Aesthetics and Politics*. London and New
York: Continuum.

Ramírez, S. 2008: *El cielo llora por mí*. Madrid: Alfaguara.

—— 2001a: La operación perfecta. In *La jornada*, miércoles, 26 de
septiembre.

—— 2001b: La serpiente que se muerde la cola. Managua, enero 2001,
http://www.sergioramirez.com/site_sergio/articulos/
laserpiente.htm

—— 2000: Reencuentro habanero con Sergio Ramírez. In *Casa de las
Américas* 219: 134–9.

References

—— 1999: *Adiós muchachos. Una memoria de la revolución sandinista*, México, D.F.: Aguilar.

—— 1998b: Literatura y el lado oculto de la historia. Claudia Pérez Salinas. *SIEMPRE*, Sección Cultura, 2353: Julio 23.

—— 1988: *Castigo divino*, La Habana: Casa de las Américas, 1988.

—— 1987: *Las armas del futuro*. Habana: Editorial Ciencias Sociales.

—— 1986: *Estás en Nicaragua*. Managua: Editorial Nueva Nicaragua.

—— 1983: *Balcanes y volcanes y otros ensayos y trabajos*. Managua: Editorial Nueva Nicaragua.

Reber, D. 2016: *Coming to Our Senses: Affect and Order of Things for Global Culture*. New York: Columbia University Press.

Reinert, H. 2015: Sacrifice. In *Environmental Humanities* 7: 255–8.

Rey Rosa, R. *Fábula asiática*. Madrid: Alfaguara.

—— 2012: *Los sordos*. Madrid: Alfaguara.

—— 2009: *El material humano*. Barcelona: Anagrama.

—— 2008: *Siempre juntos y otros cuentos*. Mexico City: Alamadía.

—— 2007: *Otro zoo*. Barcelona: Seix Barral.

—— 2006: *Caballeriza*. Barcelona: Seix Barral.

—— 1999: *La orilla africana*. Barcelona: Seix Barral.

—— 1998: *Ningún lugar sagrado*. Barcelona: Seix Barral.

—— 1996: *El cojo bueno*. Madrid: Alfaguara.

—— 1994: *Lo que soñó Sebastián*. Barcelona: Seix Barral.

—— 1992: *Cárcel de árboles*. Barcelona: Seix Barral.

González-Rivera. V. 2014: The Alligator Woman's Tale: Remembering Nicaragua's 'First Self-Declared Lesbian', *Journal of Lesbian Studies*, 18: 75–87.

Rodríguez, A. P. 2009: "La producción cultural en Centroamérica bajo la égida del neoliberalismo", in *Estudios culturales Centroamericanos en el nuevo milenio*. G. Baeza Ventura and M. Zimmerman (eds) San José: Universidad de Costa Rica.

Rodríguez, I. 2006: Globalización y gobernabilidad: Desmovilización del gestor social nacional en Centroamérica. *Istmo* 13, http://istmo.denison.edu/n13/articulos/globalizacion.html

Rubin, G. S. 1984: Thinking sex: notes for a radical theory of the politics of sexuality. In C. Vance, *Pleasure and Danger: Exploring female sexuality*. Boston: Routledge and Kegan Paul, 267–319.

Ruiz Puga, D. 2000: Panorama del texto literario en Belice, de tiempos coloniales a tiempos post-coloniales. *Istmo* 1, http://istmo.denison.edu/n01/articulos/panorama.html

—— 1995: *¡Got Seif de Cuin!*, Guatemala: Nueva Narrativa.

Sagot, M. 2013: Memoria descartada y sufrimiento invisibilizado. La violencia política de los años 40 vista desde el hospital psiquiátrico. *Revista paquidermo*, October.

http://www.revistapaquidermo.com/archives/9355

Tanke, J. 2011: *Jacques Rancière: An Introduction*. London: Continuum.

The Dawn of the Planet of the Apes 2014: Dir. M. Reeves, 20th Century Fox, DVD.

The Bible (King James version).
https://www.kingjamesbibleonline.org/Genesis-1-26/

Ugarte, E. 2001: El lenguaje y la realidad social de *Managua, Salsa City*. In *Istmo* 3, http://www.denison.edu/collaborations/istmo/n03/articulos/lenguaje.html

Urbina, N. 2004: *Violence and Structure in Margarita, Está linda la mar de Sergio Ramírez*. In *Revista Iberoamericana*, 70(207): 359–69.

Villalobos, C. M. 2003: Castígame con tus deseos. Los umbrales de Managua en la novelística de Aguirre y Galich. In *Revista Intersedes* 4 (6): 125–33.

Wacome, K. 2003: The Bible, Visual Texts and 'Outsideness': Rembrandt, Caravaggio, and Chagall on Genesis 22. http://home.nwciowa.edu/wacome/kwacome2003. html, accessed 21 June, 2015.

Weineck, S-M. 2014: *The Tragedy of Fatherhood: King Laius and the Politics of Paternity in the West*. New York: Bloomsbury Academic.

Wieser, D. 2005: Masculinidad y violencia de género en la novela negro-criminal nicaragüense. In *Badebec* 4 (8): 205–232.

White, H. 1986: Historical Pluralism. In *Critical Inquiry* 12 (3): 480–93.

Williams, R. 1977: *Marxism and Literature*. Oxford: Oxford University Press.

Young, I. M. 2005: *On Female Bodily Experience: 'Throwing Like a Girl' and Other Essays*. Oxford: Oxford University Press.

Zavala, M. 1990: La nueva novela centroamericana. Estudio de las tendencias más relevantes del género a la luz de diez novelas del período 1970–1985. Université Catholique de Louvain. Doctoral Thesis.

Žižek, S. 2012a: The Animal Gaze of the Other. In S. Žižek and B. Gunjevic. *God in Pain: Inversions of Apocalypse*. Seven Stories Press.

Žižek, S. 2012b: *Less Than Nothing: Hegel and the Shadow of Dialectical Materialism*. London: Verso.

Žižek, S. 1994: S. Žižek (ed.) *Mapping Ideology*, London: Verso.

Index

180

Index

Index

Index